I0475643

Authorpreneurship: the business of authoring, marketing and publishing your work. You actively participate in the planning, implementation and evaluation of the process to create your book, eBook, blog, editorial, whitepaper or article and its distribution as a partner or independent publisher:

Authorpreneurship:
The Business Start-Up Manual for Authors

ARE YOU A
SUPER AUTHOR?

14 Stories of Super Authors Who
Have Mastered Authorpreneurship

COMPILED BY BESTSELLING AUTHOR

SHARON C. JENKINS

DEDICATION

I dedicate this book to Jan B. King, one of my publishing heroes, who passed away on January 15, 2015. Though I only knew her for a moment, her sincere effort to better the lives of everyone she came in contact with touched me greatly.

Jan B. King was a publisher-turned-coach with over twenty-five years in the publishing industry. She was president and CEO of Merritt Publishing for eight years, doubling its revenue until they sold the company in 1998. She had fifty employees, and published over two hundred books each year and sold hundreds of thousands of copies.

In 1997, Merritt Publishing was named the forty-fourth largest woman-owned/run business in Los Angeles by the *Los Angeles Business Journal*. She was also a member of Vistage (a membership organization for CEOs) for six years, and cofounded a women's CEO group.

She authored three books, *Business Plans to Game Plans*, *Smart Women Publish*, and *Authorsmarts*, and was a long-time member of the exclusive Author's Guild.

She cofounded eWomenPublishingNetwork in 2004, an organization devoted to transforming women who are experts in their fields into successfully published authors. Through this program and independent consulting and coaching, she helped well over two hundred people become authors over the past ten years, both with established commercial publishers and by self-publishing.

She has been quoted on business and publishing in *Working Woman Magazine*, the American Bar Association's *Bar Leader* magazine, *Small Business USA*, *Business Finance*, the *Los Angeles Business Journal*, and on business websites such as WebHire. com, Office.com, YBN.com, and Portera.com. She also appeared on *Making It!*, a small business television program on KTTV Los Angeles, *The Economic Journal*, a PBS business program, and on numerous nationally syndicated business radio programs.

She founded the Virtual Author's Assistant Training Program in 2007. Prior to that she left the publishing industry to be a mom-preneur. Her passion to help authors was the catalyst that caused her to start the training program. It kept her busy making great money and doing something she loved: working with authors. She created this course using her many years of publishing and business experience and her ten years' experience as a work-from-home mom. She held nothing back and put into the course everything she'd done to create a successful, fun, lucrative home-based business for herself. She loved her work and ran a thriving, successful home-based business for several years. Over the last few years, she literally trained hundreds of people to be virtual author's assistants. But they became more to her than trainees—they became family.

TABLE of CONTENTS

ACKNOWLEDGEMENTS

I would like to personally thank the Ellechor Media team for their support and commitment to making this book the jewel that it is.

FOREWORD

With the growth spurt of small independent publishing houses and self-publishing options, there has been much debate over recent years on what a *real* author looks like. Is it getting one traditional book deal, or are you real only after you receive your first positive book review? Is it the positive review from a notable reviewer that seals you in as an "author to watch," or the big advance check that allows authors to go from unreal to real?

The real truth is that anyone who publishes a book, no matter the method or the quality, is an author. The only distinction to be seen to date is whether or not an author has chosen to make writing their lifestyle and their business. Being an author requires a significant investment, from the time spent researching unique novel perspectives and perfecting one's writing abilities, to launching events and promotions. As writers take the plunge into authorship, the reminder of what is truly necessary to be successful is a critical part of their development into entrepreneurs.

A REAL Authorpreneur is someone who is Relevant, Entrepreneurial, Action-Oriented, and Literary-Focused.

— Sharon C. Jenkins

I'd like to take that a step further and expound on that a bit, REAL authorpreneurs are:

Relevant—The worst thing an aspiring author can say is that "they don't read much." What? To be a relevant author, you must know what is going on in your industry and genre. It is critical for writers to be well-read, or they will find that their books completely miss the mark on any ideas they are trying to express. Whether you are writing fiction or nonfiction, you should know your industry and those who are successful in the craft you crave.

Writers are readers. Read widely, and don't forget to go back to the classics regularly.
– Sharon Norris Elliott

Entrepreneurial—In addition to remaining relevant through reading, authors must remain relevant through training. Every entrepreneur invests in their business and seeks out the latest information and the newest trends, studying to show themselves approved. Authorpreneurs put their entrepreneurial hat on, develop Book Business Plans™ and marketing plans, and devise a publishing strategy to ensure their success.

In order for others to be willing to invest in you, you must first invest in yourself. You are asking readers to invest in your product; attend conferences, take writing workshops, study the industry and your genre. This will keep you in contact with what's going on in the industry, and make you worthy of their investment.
– Rochelle Carter

Action-oriented—Real authorpreneurs are not simply data gatherers—they are doers. Every story you will find in this book is based on one thing: *action*. Knowledge without action is useless and produces zero results. As you read this book, pay attention to the specific action-oriented steps each author has taken which boosted their career to the next level.

Authors who understand the importance of establishing multiple promotional platforms, honing their communication skills, and identifying multiple sales vehicles—all key components of an authorpreneur's arsenal—will be the people who survive the ebb and flow of this volatile industry.
– Brian W. Smith

Literary-focused—This should be a given for any aspiring or seasoned writer, so I'll consider this a simple reminder. Perfect your craft. Study your writing style. Read. Give back to the literary community whenever you can.

This fascinating read compiled by The Master Communicator™ and bestselling author Sharon Jenkins takes us behind the scenes of authors who have embraced their entrepreneurial personas to enhance their appeal to readers. They have enhanced the literary landscape not only with their publications but with their wisdom and their commitment to remaining literary-focused and business-minded.

As you read these accounts of real authorpreneurship, ask yourself, *Are you ready to stand up and stand out?*

Rochelle Carter, CEO of Ellechor Media, LLC

INTRODUCTION

I have been intrigued by two sisters, Red and Black (Tina Pennington and Mandy Williams), ever since I heard them speak at a NAWBO (National Association of Women Business Owners) luncheon in August 2010. Their book had been launched the prior August by Neiman Marcus, and I was fascinated by their business story—the story of how Black turned her sister's personal crisis into a new business venture, the foundation of which is their self-published book, *What I Learned About Life When My Husband Got Fired!*

I hoped I would be able to convince them to consider speaking at my 2010 Author's Summit, so I contacted them through their website.[1] Looking back, I wish I had thought to videotape their presentation.

The first thing they did was ask me lots of questions. But I guess I should have expected that—Red will be the first to tell you that when she turned to her sister after her husband got fired, she was looking for answers. And sympathy.

She got neither. Instead, she got lots of questions.

So did I.

The sisters wanted to better understand what I was trying to achieve with my Author's Summit, what my motivation was, and who the audience was going to be before they would make a decision. I realize now that they wanted to make sure there was a good fit—that doing speaking engagements for uninterested audiences is not a good use of anyone's time (Lesson 1).

I guess I must have given them the "right" answers because they agreed to speak, although there was no budget for paying speaker fees and I had no idea the size of the audience. I told them they could have a table to sell their books at the event, but, surprisingly, they chose not to. At the time I thought that an unusual decision, but after hearing them speak at NAWBO, I realized many of their decisions are unusual (Lesson 2: sometimes you have to think differently than the rest).

The sisters took all my "correct" answers and developed a presentation proposal they thought would be of interest to the Summit attendees. They told me what they would talk about, which was the basis for their handout to the audience, detailing the chronology/history of their business and their book. Their presentation was entitled "*Red & Black … and Their Informative 'Story': A Roadmap for Beginning Authors.*"

I learned from their keynote speech that "truth in advertising" is a very important detail (Lesson 3). Did their presentation live up to expectations? Yes and no. Was it a roadmap, as the title indicated? Not really. But that was what made it so valuable. It discussed the many decisions that authors face when trying to decide if/how/when to publish. The decisions Red and Black had made demonstrated that each author will have different issues driving their decisions.

It was no ordinary presentation, and what I think I and the attendees of the Author's Summit walked away with were five main points, although there were many more.

One, do your homework. Prior to starting on the business plan for "Red & Black," Black researched the entertainment industry extensively and, in particular, the publishing world in order to better understand the business model, the competition, and the market. Although her background was in the oil and gas industry, she knew a well-developed business plan and marketing strategy was critical regardless of the industry or specific project. A book, unless it is written merely for personal pleasure or as a hobby, needs to be evaluated just as you would any other business venture or product.

Two, have realistic objectives. Red explained, rolling her eyes and laughing, that she is the warm and fuzzy one, whereas Black is extremely pragmatic and even manages to look at relationships without emotional bias. However, Black made her realize in terms of personal decisions (whether it be financial or related to things like time management, handling stress, or any other "Life 101" topic), one's goals and objectives must be realistic—they need to make you strive, but they must also be obtainable. The key is to set yourself up for success, not failure.

Three, make decisions based on your values and priorities. The subtitle of the sisters' book is "A Real Approach to Personal Finance and Prioritizing Your Life." The concept of having your values and priorities drive all your decisions (financial and otherwise) sounds obvious—but sometimes is easier said than done. As an example, Red and Black made a decision to print in the United States, although it cost twice as much as printing in China. Black explained how, if they had based their decision solely on the numbers, it would have been a very easy decision to make. But she did not want to send her money to China, and even went so far to ask the domestic printer to "defend" their pricing; as expected, some of the additional expense was related to labor costs, though some of it was due to US regulations in terms of environmental laws and workers safety. Black reminded us that there is a price for maintaining high standards, and in business—and life—often there are times where you must decide if your words and actions will match.

Four, learn when to be reactive instead of proactive. Until their book was launched, Red and Black were extremely proactive. However, all that changed when they started getting feedback from actual readers. They initially thought their market was Baby Boomer women, but the book was resonating with men and women of all ages. And then they were asked to develop a personal finance program for KIPP Houston High School. If they had looked at their original marketing strategy as etched in stone, as many authors (and entrepreneurs) do, Red and Black would not have even considered the detour. But although the book had only just been released, they decided to stop marketing and start working on lesson plans. In fact, soon after they spoke at my Author's Summit, their book was approved by the Texas State Board of Education as a financial literacy textbook—not something they ever considered. But the very latest detour sounds more like a movie script … they have gone to prison. Well, technically, their book has gone to prison, as it is now the basis of the "Red & Black Personal Finance & Life 101 Program" being used by the Chaplaincy Department of the Texas Department of Criminal Justice.

Five, long-term planning is backward thinking. This concept is initially discussed in their book, where Red wants to start planning for the future and explains to Black how she's standing here today and thinking about what she needs/wants to do in the days, months, and even years ahead. Black's reaction is to explain how her approach is very different. This approach, and the mindset that drives it, ended up becoming the theme of their NAWBO presentation, and applies not only to "how to write a book" or business in general but to one's life. Black explains it as thinking about where you want to be and what you want to accomplish, and then working backward. Doing so will help you make decisions along the way because you will be able to see whether today's decisions are taking you down the path to your final destination or not. If, along the way, you hit a roadblock or a detour, stop—think about where you want to go. Then, as stated in the sisters' presentation proposal, realize "there are many different roads to the same destination and [that] you have to be prepared for detours and/or road blocks, but they don't mean you cannot reach your destination … and maybe even find a better way."

It now has been years since I first met "Red & Black," and I have been watching their brand expand into so many different areas. Their demographic has now been proven to cover men and women ranging from middle school students to senior citizens, across all socioeconomic strata.

When I asked Black whether that surprised her, she of course answered with a question … and asked me why I thought that had happened. My response was that Red & Black must be providing something that people either want or need or both.

Her response? Another question. She asked me what I thought that want or need might be. I thought about it, and said that people love stories. People do not learn from being told what to do but from the wisdom and success of others—which has to be told in such a way that people not only relate to but can walk away from it with something they can apply in their own life and/or business.

Determined to get Black to actually answer a question, I then said I wanted to include a description not only of her but of her sister so that people would have a better understanding of their areas of expertise—though I wanted it from her perspective.

She explained that Red is a self-proclaimed warm-and-fuzzy fulltime mom, and that Black credits her sister's "crisis" with forcing Red to learn to take control of her life versus letting her life control her. Most importantly, Red has been able to share those life lessons (ranging from personal finance to time management to handling stress to planning for the future) with her daughters.

Conveniently, Black did not describe herself. So I asked her if the description of her on the book jacket was still accurate, hoping to get some new insight. (I have to admit, she is the only woman I have ever met who races Ferraris.)

Instead, she quoted the disclaimer from the book: "We are real people. We are not claiming to be experts in any given field, but rather are becoming experts of our own lives."

I have often said that the meaning of authorpreneurship is an author who guides and actively participates in the business process of authoring, marketing, and publishing their work. But I believe it is essential that they also exhibit a servant-leader's heart in helping others to do likewise. Black made me realize that if we let other people decide what they can learn from us versus trying to convince people we are experts that are going to teach them something, it might create opportunities for discussion and sharing of ideas. When I laughingly said, "You really like to make people stop and think, don't you?", she merely said, "Yes."

I realized, in that one word, that she had finally given me the insight that I had been looking for—that we should all stop … and think.

Ironically enough, that may be the greatest lesson of all.

If you remember the old television series *To Tell the Truth*, you are vaguely familiar with the line, "Will the *real* _____ please stand up?" For those of you who don't know, three different participants on the show were pretending to be the same person, and the panel had to determine which one of the imposters was the *real* person whose life story was being told.

In today's publishing world, because of the electronic development called the e-book and with self-publishing becoming an acceptable means for marketing a book, things have certainly changed for authors. Anyone, and I mean anyone, can become an author—it's just a matter of pushing a button. But if you really want to know who the *real* authors are, you will need some form of measuring tool.

This book seeks to provide one of those tools.

Since we live in a world of predominantly visual learners—and I truly respect that—I am offering you a show-and-tell day in the School of Authorpreneurship in this book. I have gathered personal stories from thirteen REAL authorpreneurs like Red and Black, to share with you, those authors who have proven over time that they are Relevant, Entrepreneurial, Action-oriented, and Literary-focused. In addition, they have all in some way, shape, or form dedicated a part of their journey to helping other authors. Each one describes in detail how they started out, where they are now, and what budding authorpreneurs should do in order to have similar success.

If you desire a rewarding journey similar to theirs, then get into your favorite reading chair and cuddle up with a book that promises to be educating, empowering, and entertaining.

Happy writing,
Sharon C. Jenkins, The Master Communicator

Joel Friedlander is an award-winning book designer, blogger, and the author of *A Self-Publisher's Companion: Expert Advice for Authors Who Want to Publish* and *The Self-Publisher's Ultimate Resource Guide.* He's been launching the careers of self-publishers since 1994 and writes TheBookDesigner.com, a popular blog on book design, book marketing, and the future of the book. Joel is also the founder of the online training course "The Self-Publishing Roadmap" and a former president of the Bay Area Independent Publishers Association.

Contact him on Twitter @JFBookman.

CHAPTER ONE
ON BECOMING AN AUTHORPRENEUR

Joel Friedlander

Growing up as the son of a printer instilled an early love in me for type fonts and their use through the art of typography and its practical expression in the graphic arts. There were huge catalogs from the American Type Foundry around our house, and I spent many happy hours looking at all the different ways the same words could be typeset to produce radically different looks for different uses.

Although I didn't have a model in my family for how to be an entrepreneur, at some point I started to wonder how *I could make a difference in the world*. I developed a love for writing and, eventually, for books themselves. This started a lifelong love affair with book publishing and the graphic arts. Since I'm also a writer, it was inevitable that these two streams would eventually converge—on the one hand, my wanting to make a contribution, and on the other, my interest in book publishing.

In a sense I was following the same path that many self-publishing authors had traveled before me. Before the introduction of print-on-demand and e-book publishing, virtually every self-publisher was an entrepreneur of one kind or another. You had to be an "authorpreneur" (although I don't think that term came into fashion until quite recently) in order to be a self-publisher.

For a long time, there were only three paths open if you wanted to publish a book:

1. Submit your manuscript to agents or editors and try to obtain a publishing contract with a traditional publisher

2. Contract with a "vanity" publisher (we now call these "subsidy" publishers) who would publish your book for a hefty fee

3. Start your own publishing company, hire the vendors you needed, and publish the book yourself

4. It was within this context that I first started self-publishing.

At the time, I had access to some specialized information that would be of great interest to only a small population of potential book buyers. Since I was working in the publishing industry at the time, I was keenly aware that a book with a very small potential readership simply was not of interest to publishers. Since I knew all the people I would need—

typesetters, book printers, proofreaders, and so on—I decided to start a company to publish my books.

I soon found that book publishing was a perfect amalgam of these two impulses that drove me, one the authorial impulse to write and share what I knew, the other the entrepreneurial impulse to create something new in the world to bring these books to as many readers as possible. I formed Globe Press Books, and the rest of my career flowed from that initial decision.

Today, I've fulfilled both those impulses and gone far beyond my original vision largely because of the developments that have taken place in the interim between when I began in the 1980s and now. The two most prominent of these developments relate to digitization and the wide ranging effects it has had on industry and society. First is the appearance of the Internet, and second the development of print-on-demand technology.

All of us appreciate how the Internet and the growth of the online world has changed society and commerce, and I'll get to the way it changed my own business in a moment. But the rise of print-on-demand was pivotal in the explosion of self-publishing authors because it *removed the risk* involved in publishing print books.

Before print-on-demand (and the reason that virtually all self-publishers were entrepreneurs in the old days), anyone who wanted to publish a book faced the serious risk of having to invest thousands of dollars in an unproven consumer product—their book. You had to pay all the norm-al development costs associated with book publishing, from hiring editors and artists to proofreaders and marketing help. Beyond that, though, was the printing bill. And book printers in general don't extend credit, so you had to pay the entire invoice before you even had a product to sell. This kept most authors out of self-publishing.

Now, with print-on-demand, there's no need to fill your garage with stacks of cartons containing your books. No need to buy a hand truck to take orders down to the local post office for shipping. No need to save up to pay that printer's bill.

This has allowed me and tens of thousands of other authors to put our work out into the market, and vastly expanded the choices for consumers.

Following these developments, I decided in 2009 to start a blog based on my experience with book design, production, publishing, and marketing, all gained during years of publishing my own books and running a book design business that catered to small- to medium-sized book publishers.

My blog quickly became popular because there wasn't anyone else writing about the details of book construction, the rules and guidelines behind the detailed decisions one has to make when you decide to publish a book, or the most effective ways to approach the publishing process. As an entrepreneur, I recognized this as a real market opening, an opportunity to establish an online asset that might one day pay dividends.

To establish my blog as a trusted authority site, I wrote in a friendly, conversational style, paid a lot of attention to the visitors who started to trickle in, and began developing a lot of content aimed at these visitors and their needs. As the blog grew, I began looking for ways to make it into more of a business, not just a hobby. I think my own development as an author, blogger, publisher, and internet marketer are due to the efforts I made along these lines over the last five years.

Seeing opportunities in the market and seizing them to bring your message, product, or service to a wider audience is the essence of entrepreneurship. Doing it with books is what makes you an "authorpreneur."

I've found that it's becoming easier and easier—especially for nonfiction authors—to use the incredible tools we have available online to fulfill this entrepreneurial impulse. Here are some of the ways I've found to use my entrepreneurial energy to grow my book publishing beyond the scope of what we usually think of as "being an author":

- Realizing that *education* was the most powerful aspect of what I was doing on my blog, I started to take a more studied approach to what I was writing, and the result was a collection of e-books based on blog articles, each focusing on a specific area I knew writers were having trouble with: copyright, ISBN issues, print-on-demand, and book distribution.

Over the years these have expanded my reach, and they continue to sell every day from my site.

- This desire to educate also led to the publication of *A Self-Publisher's Companion: Expert Advice for Authors Who Want to Publish.*[1] This book, widely praised throughout the industry, grew out of about forty blog posts that were edited and reformatted to create the book.

- Later I began to experiment with translating some of my written content into different media. Creating audio and video content allowed me to reach even more people, and these skills came into play as I continued to expand.

- Early on I started participating enthusiastically in social media and built a following on Twitter, which grew to become a major traffic stream for my blog and other activities.

- After experimenting with live events, I started making public appearances to talk about all the same subjects I had been developing on my blog. Again, this was another outreach to different audiences than those I had been able to contact online.

- Many of these efforts came together when I started offering webinars and teleseminars—live online educational events. I can still remember the very first webinar I ever ran, and the slightly terrifying but mysterious fact that I could sit in front of my computer in northern California and talk to it while being heard by dozens of people around the world.

- Eventually I began studying internet marketing in earnest. I realized that *all authors who sell online are, in fact, internet marketers.*

- Taking all these skills, I created a video-based training course to teach authors about book publishing. "The Self-Publishing Roadmap" is the result and has been a great financial boost to my other activities.[2] (It's a lot easier to create profit with an $897 course than it is with an $8.97 book.)

- Eventually I moved into selling digital products that would help authors get their books done faster, better, and cheaper. I founded BookDesignTemplates.com, and now this e-commerce site produces a good percentage of my monthly income.

- This year I went back to the well again to team up with traditional publishing legend Betty Sargent to publish *The Self-Publisher's Ultimate Resource Guide*, filling another hole in the market.[3] Launching as a No. 1 Amazon bestseller in its category, it has been highly recommended by many in the industry.

- I continued to ramp up my speaking and consulting events, activities that now bring in a substantial percentage of monthly income.

- All this started with my original blog, TheBookDesigner.com, which is still the "hub" of my online activities.

I think what all this shows is that even in a very small market like indie publishing, someone with information to communicate and a willingness to try new things can build a very profitable business based solely on the product of your own mind and your ability to work hard to realize your opportunities.

Back in the 1980s, it was challenging to find anyone who wanted to talk about type fonts, book publishing, or book design. Now, when I publish an article to my blog or create a compelling piece of audio or video content, I know it will be seen by tens of thousands of people around the world.

Is there any better motivation for combining your own writing with the entrepreneurial spirit?

Writing Alchemy: How to Write Fast and Deep, four anthologies of award-winning stories entitled *Seasons of Our Lives: Spring, Summer, Autumn, Winter*, and the collective memoir *Rosie's Daughters: The "First Woman To" Generation Tells Its Story* all draw on **Matilda Butler's** fifty years of research training and work experiences. In addition to being an award-winning and bestselling Kindle author, she is a social psychologist, authorpreneur, conference presenter, and memoir coach with a passion for helping others tell their stories in powerful and engaging ways.

Matilda taught and conducted research at Stanford University, published a hundred-plus articles and book chapters about women in work and education, created the nationwide Women's Educational Equity Communication Network, and cofounded Knowledge Access International, a software company specializing in CD-ROM information products. After selling the company, she returned to research and writing, which resulted in *Rosie's Daughters*, the story of the generation of women born during WWII shaped by the '60s who didn't take "no" for an answer. Her experiences with *Rosie's Daughters* led to teaching memoir writing, founding WomensMemoirs.com, and developing her student-tested, award-winning system called Writing Alchemy.

Matilda moved to Oregon in 2010 and currently splits her writing time between Corvallis and Waikoloa Beach.

Contact her at WomensMemoirs.com or on Twitter @rosiesbandana.

CHAPTER TWO

YOU CAN BE AN AUTHORPRENEUR...REALLY

Matilda Butler

What? I know you may still be working on writing your book, but now you realize you need to be an authorpreneur. It can sound overwhelming, so let's start with the fun part.

Imagine this.

It's May 30, a warm, sunny, late afternoon in Los Angeles. You arrive at the Miyako Hotel, unpack, put on your finery, comb your hair, add red lipstick and a touch of blush, and catch a cab to the Wells Fargo Building. The elevator takes you to the fifty-fourth floor, where you see that the lights of the city are beginning to twinkle through the large window panels as the sun sets. The reason for your visit? You're receiving a national book award, an IPPY.

You know why you're there, but still you have an unexpected and more-than-ample supply of butterflies in your stomach and your hands are a little sweaty. Then the thrill when the emcee announces in a booming voice, "And the winner is ... " Suddenly you are at the front of the room, not sure how you managed to walk up there. Everyone is clapping. The emcee puts the medal around your neck and shakes your damp hand. You even manage to hold your book so that the cover shows clearly. Photographs capture the moment.

IT'S ALL PART OF BEING AN AUTHORPRENEUR

Are you amazed this happened? Do you say "I can't believe this?" Or perhaps "I don't deserve this?" No. Getting a book award doesn't just happen. The world doesn't decide to clap for all your hard work on its own. Readers, or potential readers, don't line up to purchase your book mysteriously. I like the way Sharon Jenkins addresses this point in her book *Authorpreneurship: The Business Start-Up Manual for Authors*. She has an entire chapter entitled, "If I Write It, They Will Come ... Or Not." Writing success requires a plan you put into place, your plan as an authorpreneur.

And yes, that's me receiving an IPPY (and eventually three other book awards) for my collective memoir, *Rosie's Daughters: The "First Woman To" Generation Tells Its Story*. I had even practiced how to hold the book so that the cover would show up in photographs. Small details that lead to success take planning and effort.

And how do you become an authorpreneur? Rochelle Carter, in her book *The 7-Step Guide to Authorpreneurship*, points to a key concept when she notes that being an authorpreneur is a state of mind. She goes on to say that you need to have it,

> ... before, during, and even after you have a book released. It doesn't matter if you decide to publish independently (go "indie") or traditionally, or if you want to handle marketing for the book on your own or hire a publicist instead. The mindset is still the same: *you* are determining and handling your writing career—your way.[1]

BECOMING AN AUTHORPRENEUR: MY STORY

This part of the tale begins with *Rosie's Daughters*, a collective memoir of American women born during World War II, precursors of the Baby Boom generation.

Rosie the Riveter is a mythic figure in our culture, with good reason—she built ships, flew bombers, and filled thousands of other essential wartime jobs, upending traditional views of "women's work." When the war was over, however, American industry thanked Rosie and merely sent her home. Rosie's "daughters," however, grew up and flung wide the doors of employment opportunity that Rosie had unlocked. These women can claim more career "firsts" and greater sociocultural change than any other generation.

I'm a "Rosie's daughter," and my tale began after attending the fortieth reunion of my high school class. In one session, we were seated around tables in the cavernous room where four decades earlier I had studied English Lit, American History, French, and Algebra every afternoon and evening. Representatives of each quinquennial reunion class spoke about their experiences, telling stories that were alternatively humorous and serious because of the momentous times in which we all have lived. I was struck by how the stories of my class differed from those of women who graduated even five years earlier or later.

Once back in my California home, my thoughts often returned to that session. For the most part, despite good educations, women who graduated earlier than my class did not seek careers but found fulfillment as wives, mothers, and homemakers. Women who graduated some years after my class (Baby Boomers, Gen Xers, Millennials), on the other hand, took their careers and the juggling act of work and family for granted. They were fulfilling a pattern they had observed and planned for.

My generation had a much more complicated and even confused story to tell. When we were in high school, we expected to spend our lives in traditional roles. Sometime after that—in fact, at different times for different reasons— unprecedented numbers of women born during WWII switched tracks and pursued careers. None of us remember thinking, *Well, of course that's what I'll do*. Instead, we opened closed doors and moved in what seemed to be the right direction until the next door appeared, then repeated the process. By trial and error, we became proficient in careers that we never imagined. Combining careers and children presented novel challenges, but we were young and energetic. I assumed we were among the role models that the younger alumnae observed, inspiring them to think, *Well, of course that's what I'll do.*

I wanted to determine how well this model held up across my generation of war babies. What I found was a story of women that begged to be told, though not in the way that I originally envisioned. When I started work on the book, I saw myself as a social psychologist writing a research-based nonfiction account of a generation of women. By the time I completed the interviews of women across America, I had become a memoirist, helping a generation of women tell their stories in a collective memoir.

Along the way I found a coauthor (a longtime colleague, Kendra Bonnett), an editor, a publisher, and a terrific book designer. The marketing and merchandising that followed on the heels of the publication of *Rosie's Daughters* (now in its second edition) has been as explosive as the book itself. Through our blog at RosiesDaughters.com and through social networking on Twitter,[2] Facebook,[3] and Pinterest,[4] Kendra and I have connected with thousands of women.

Did I mention merchandising? To make book presentations and book signings livelier, I wanted to wear a red and white polka dot bandana just like Rosie wore. I searched the Internet and couldn't find anything like the authentic one, which had a random pattern of large polka dots. I thought about making one, but there wasn't even a fabric that would work. So I had a graphic designer create the pattern and commissioned a few silk-screened bandanas. After presentations, people asked, "Where can I get one like that?" and wanted to purchase one like mine, so I sold the extras I had made. The ones I had quickly sold out, and soon I was getting twelve hundred bandanas at a time. Today, I order in batches of three thousand and have fabric dyed exclusively for us. Kendra and I sell thousands of these bandanas every year to women who want to make a statement about their own sense of empowerment. It's a most gratifying connection. We sell our entire product line through Etsy.com.

But *Rosie's Daughters* had legs that went beyond merchandise. Its publication brought me into the larger sphere of memoir writing and its importance as a literary genre.

Telling personal stories is a valuable form of healing for many writers and storytellers. It's also a source of inspiration, encouragement, and insight for readers. Kendra and I launched our blogsite Women'sMemoirs.com in February 2008, and today—more than one thousand posts later—we are connecting with thousands of people each month. This started us on our path of working with memoir writers, both published and aspiring. Now we teach, coach, and consult on writing and book marketing.

And yes, we also developed products for memoirists— teas for writers, Thai silk journals made exclusively for us, mugs with inspirational messages, and more. I took videos of my all-day memoir writing workshops and turned them into a product with twenty-one video lessons; this let us reach a much broader audience than possible when only teaching in person. And the list goes on.

After four years of workshops, online classes, live events, coaching, and speaking about writing, Kendra and I undertook the book that would address many of the problems that we saw our students have. We had developed a new conceptual framework that became *Writing Alchemy: How to Write Fast and Deep.*[5]

AUTHORPRENEURSHIP INCLUDES WRITING, PUBLISHING, MARKETING, AND...

Like Rosie the Riveter, authorpreneurs have a "We can do it" attitude. And that's what you need in today's marketplace. Publishing—indeed most industries—are experiencing dramatic change. At first blush the changes appear to cause more chaos than opportunity. But with an open mind, an aggressive can-do attitude, and a willingness to embrace change and make it work, we can more than survive the turmoil; we can make it work to our advantage.

In the case of publishing, with cash advances having all but vanished, with the disappearance and consolidation of many older publishing firms, and with the very real problem of being discovered when traditional bookstores go out of business, we also have many new opportunities—the rise of e-books, social media, and print-on-demand publishing and bookselling juggernauts like Amazon. We have exciting new ways to make our mark.

We have much more flexibility than ever, and by publishing yourself, no one is going to control your product. Put it out there, build your platform, market yourself, create a following. It can take a while to break through, but if you have something readers/customers want, you can generate a following. Or if you decide to go with a small- or mid-sized publisher—actually any publisher—you'll find that the more you bring to the table, the more of an authorpreneur you are, the more successful you will be with the additional assistance of a publisher.

If you have an idea, a dream, a passion, follow it … even if it's never been done before. Be the first.

Brian W. Smith is the award-winning, bestselling author of fourteen novels, including *HOARDER, DEADBEAT, Nina's Got a Secret, If These Trees Could Talk,* and *The Audubon Park Murder.* His novels have earned spots on the Dallas Morning News, Amazon, and Black Expressions Bestsellers lists. He has been awarded the Male Author of the Year by several literary organizations (AALBC and OOSA Reviewers, to name a few), and he's cohost of The Bookends radio show.

Brian's educational background includes Bachelor's Degrees in Business Administration and Criminal Justice, and a Master of Business Administration. When Brian is not writing novels, traveling to literary events, and meeting with book clubs nationwide, he serves as an Adjunct Professor of Creative Writing at a community college in the Dallas, Texas, area.

Brian is a native of New Orleans, Louisiana, and currently resides in McKinney, Texas.

Contact him at AuthorBrianWSmith.com
or bws@authorbrianwsmith.com.

CHAPTER THREE
AUTHORPRENEURSHIP: I DID IT MY WAY

Brian W. Smith

"Authorpreneurship," the bastard love child of two words (author and entrepreneurship) that were once taboo to mention in the same sentence. A mythical word that was more elusive than Bigfoot or the Loch Ness Monster. A word that once moved "real" writers (those scribes who spout Shakespeare while pecking away on antique typewriters) to deem anyone audacious enough to utter the word as a low-life cheater of the writing craft who deserved to perish under a pile of publishing house rejection letters.

Oh, but how times have changed. Fortunately for me, the change started to take place shortly after I entered this literary industry in 2006—the same year a Harvard student named Zuckerberg took his social media company, Facebook, from being a restricted site and opened it up to anyone thirteen years and older with an email address.

I was a freshly minted MBA, who was naïve to the way things were done in the fickle world of publishing. My background was in business. I flaunted a corporate title, took advantage of a corporate expense account, and viewed all things business through a pair of corporate lenses. All decision making started with a SWOT Analysis and ended with a clearly defined ROI. It was a way of thinking that helped me climb the corporate ladder, and I was sure it would serve me well in the publishing industry.

Prior to penning my first manuscript, I'd never written any fiction. In fact, I could count on one hand the number of fiction books I'd ever read. My leisurely reading was reserved for books that talked about ways to earn more money, get the next promotion, and how to inspire and motivate people. Even after I released my first novel and opened my publishing company (Hollygrove Publishing), I often told anyone who asked, "I'm not a writer who owns a business. I'm a businessman who happens to write." Every time I spouted that line, "real" writers would glare at me like they wanted to stab my eyes with their dull, eraser-less pencils.

Fast forward nearly ten years. Bookstores in the United States have been closing faster than authors can trade their desktop computers in for laptops. Physical book sales (hardcover and paperback) have plummeted. More and more readers walk around with their entire inventory of books in their purses—stored safely on an electronic device that's smaller than a standard size spiral notepad. The literary industry has taken a stroll down electronic lane, and it ain't coming back—and I for one, am glad.

Why am I glad? I'll tell you. I'm glad the literary industry has become more electronic, because my skill set and authorpreneurship mentality (that used to make my peers give me the side-eye and brand me a faker) is no longer viewed as a curse. In fact, my background has been the primary reason I've been able to survive in this high-stress-low-profit industry.

Some authors I encounter—the ones who despise the business side of the job—hope and pray that the industry goes back to the days of five and six figure advances, publisher-sponsored book tours for midlist authors, and royalty checks that sponsor summer family vacations. I just listen to their ramblings, shaking my head pitifully. Sometimes I feel like I'm listening to a forty-year-old former high school football star going on and on about the good old days. Their eyes glaze over. Smirks creep onto their faces. Their pleasant memories can be viewed on their foreheads.

I allow them their moments. Watching them bask in the past is both entertaining and sad. I don't have the heart to tell them that things are never going to go back to the way they used to be.

The truth of the matter is no one knows for sure that things are going to go back to the way they used to be. After all, the cassette tape made a comeback ... oops, no it didn't. The VHS recorder still holds a lot of value ... my bad, that's another bad example. All jokes aside, despite all of the examples around us that once technology gets its foot into an industry there is no turning back, many authors still believe that the hardcover novel is going to make a comeback, publishers are going to once again start writing huge checks, and the need for authors to transform into authorpreneurs is going to fade away.

I for one don't believe things will change, and I have two personal experiences to back up my claim: my experience once I signed a deal with Strebor/Simon and Schuster and my job as an Adjunct Professor.

In 2012, I signed a one-book deal with Strebor/Simon and Schuster. After spending my first six years as a self-published author, it was refreshing to allow someone else take on the grunt work of producing, distributing, and promoting my novel. But a funny thing happened after I cashed my advance check—life as an author signed to a "major" wasn't, as the kids say, "all that."

Yeah, it was cool walking into a few major retail outlets and seeing my book on the shelves, but after the excitement died and it was time to get down to the business of selling books, life as a traditionally published author seemed a lot like my life as a self-published author. Marketing my book was my responsibility. Coordinating my book signings was my responsibility. Scheduling interviews on radio shows was my responsibility. Trying to figure out ways to get more readers to buy the book before retailers packaged them up in ninety days and shipped them back to the publisher—thus ruining my chance of receiving any royalty check—was ultimately my responsibility. I enjoyed the prestige that came with being able to say I had a major book deal, but it was my experiences in the world of *authorpreneurship* that enabled me to survive that not-so-pleasant time.

During the latter part of 2012, I accepted an Adjunct Professor position in the Creative Writing Division of a community college. Imagine my surprise when I wasn't asked to teach the traditional Creative Writing type classes: "How to Write a Strong Antagonist" or "How to Write in Third Person." The department coordinator asked me to teach several *authorpreneurship*-style classes. Classes with titles like: "How to Market and Promote Your Novel" and "How to Self-Publish Your Novel."

When I got the news that I'd been hired to teach those authorpreneurship-style classes, I wanted to go on one of the social media "author groups" I'm a member of and rub the news of my new teaching gig in the face of all of those "real" authors who once swore that entertaining thoughts of the business side of writing guaranteed all struggling authors a one-way trip to literary purgatory. I didn't gloat, but I did get a picture of one of my classes—filled with nearly thirty aspiring authors eager to learn the ways of the authorpreneur and posted it on social media.

As I survey the literary landscape these days, I've noticed two things: many "real" authors who refused to get off high-horses and become authorpreneurs have lost their book deals, and e-books are sending physical books the way of the dinosaur. My best advice is that authors who understand the importance of establishing multiple promotional platforms, honing their communication skills, and identifying multiple sales vehicles—all key components of an authorpreneur's arsenal—will be the people who survive the ebb and flows of this volatile industry.

"Live significantly!" is the inspiring message of **Sharon Norris Elliott**, award-winning author, speaker, and astute Bible teacher, who always encourages everyone who will listen to live a life that matters. Her three latest published books are *Why I Get Into Trouble; Boomerangs to Arrows: A Godly Guide for Launching Young Adult Children;* and *Power Suit: The Armor of God Fit for the Feminine Frame.*

Sharon is a dedicated teacher, and, in addition to her writing ministry, she's a licensed minister, popular conference and retreat speaker, and editor-in-chief of *Gospel Roads* magazine (GospelRoads.com). Sharon also instructs Christian authors, encouraging them toward excellence in the business. To that end, she teaches at major Christian writers' conferences nationwide, and is CEO of AuthorizeMe®, through which she conducts hands-on seminars, personally assisting attendees toward their publishing goals. Sharon is adding to her thirty-year career as a high school English teacher at Orange Lutheran High School in Southern California.

Sharon and her husband, James, are enjoying each other and their empty nest, left so by their blended family of five grown children, three of whom have given them their four grandchildren.

Discover more at her ministry website, LifeThatMatters.net, and devotional blog, SaneWriter.wordpress.com.

CHAPTER FOUR

MULTI-FACETED AUTHORPRENEUR

Sharon Norris Elliott

Authorpreneur—that portmanteau is the perfect synonym for my journey in the writing and speaking world. It's a world I seemed to have stumbled upon, yet I feel as though I was born to be a part of it.

As a child, I loved books. Mom signed me up for a book club when I was about nine years old. How exciting it was to receive one or two books per month addressed directly to me! Thus began my love affair both with books and one of my favorite authors, Theodore Geisel, more popularly known as Dr. Seuss. Besides crafting amazing children's stories with meaningful lessons, he had a command of the language that made words and phrases ring. I began to write poems and compose musical lyrics that I combined with my musical ability on the piano. The concert choir in which I sang— *The Voices of Joi*—incorporated some of my songs into our repertoire.

My fascination with good books and songwriting eventually combined, and I became a playwright, specifically a composer of musicals. By this point, I had graduated from Biola University and was teaching at Celeste Scott Christian School, which was founded by Mrs. Margaret Jenkins, a professional gospel singer. Every school program was a major theatrical musical production. My original productions rivaled *FAME* and could very well have been the forerunner of *Glee.* My students were so great in the musicals that I formed a company called His Kids Players. We went on the road performing scenes from the musicals at churches as the entertainment segments for various types of programs.

It was during this time, in my mid-twenties, that I became quite interested in getting married; however, as I prayed about it, God impressed upon my heart my need to be marriage material myself. I then embarked on an in-depth study of Proverbs 31:10-31 in order to internalize the qualities of the virtuous woman spoken of in the passage. Biola had supplied me with an excellent foundation in how to study the Bible, so every word went under my microscope. Once I had researched the original Hebrew meaning of each word, I put it all back together and wrote out what each verse meant.

As I went through the project, I did get married in 1985, and I started sharing my findings with my girlfriends. One day, my friend Teri Jones said, "You know, that would make a good book." I thought, *Really? That's an interesting idea,* and tucked her comment away in my mind. Then one day while driving home from work in my little red Toyota Corolla Deluxe, a radio commercial announced an upcoming Christian writers' conference that was being held close by in La Mirada, California, at Biola University, my alma mater. I checked it out and decided to attend.

The year was 1991. I had been married for six years, and my children were toddlers: Matthew was four and Mark was two years old. Looking back now, it was at this point in the story when I began to see God's hand writing the manuscript of my life as an authorpreneur. The writers' conference offered the opportunity to meet with editors and publishers from the attending publishing houses in order to present your book ideas. Wanting to present my work in an excellent manner, I printed out the pages of my Proverbs 31 Bible study and took them to Kinko's to have them bound.

While waiting for the binding to be completed, I glanced at the counter to my right. A gentleman had just collected a poster-sized mock-up of a magazine cover, which read "Christteen." When I inquired about the interesting cover, he said it was the picture of the first cover of his new publication for the African-American Christian teenager. I loved that. At the time, I was teaching at an inner city Christian high school, and my students were definitely a market for this periodical. The gentleman and I exchanged contact information, and I left the copy center with the bound copies of my Bible study.

Upon arriving at the Biola Christian Writers Conference the following week, low and behold, there was the gentleman from Kinko's. Realizing I had years of experience correcting writing, he asked me to help him with his publication. Voila! Before I even knew all that the job description really meant, I had become the managing editor of a magazine.

The rest of the conference was just as exciting. There I sat in workshops being taught by editors of foremost Christian companies and authors of books I'd read. At my fifteen-minute appointment with an editor, he looked at my Bible study and told me I had "a good start." Then he proceeded to tell me how I could improve my manuscript.

My manuscript! I thought. *Wow, he was saying that I had written a book!*

Calling my Bible study a "book" and a "manuscript" was not all I learned. What did an "acquisitions editor" do? What was included in a "book proposal"? Where was this "house" people said they worked for? "Rejection slips" sounded really horrendous, so how would I avoid them? And what the heck was a "SASE"? There was an entirely new patois in this industry and another full set of people to meet.

By the end of the conference, I realized the authors, editors, and publishers who were teaching me were letting me in on industry information I could only receive from insiders. In essence, they were training their competition. These folks were telling me all they knew about the industry, how to enter it, and how to experience success once there. That only made sense because we were working on the same team—the Christian team to get the Word of the Lord out to our dying world. I knew I wanted to be a part of this industry, so I promised the Lord that if He would allow me to be a part of this publishing world, I would give back to other aspiring authors what these people were giving me.

God took me up on my proposition.

Following this first conference was a month-long, hands-on class that promised to teach us how to write and publish a magazine article. Each week, the teachers (who had been the directors and several instructors at the conference) worked with about twenty-five of us to write, edit, polish, and then submit our articles. It took a while afterward, but not only did the article I wrote in that class ultimately get published, but to date, "Back Onto the Front Lines" has become my most frequently reprinted piece.

During the year that followed, from 1991–92, I rewrote my Bible study, turning it into a full-fledged book, and worked on building *Christteen*. Some of my students worked as writers, reporters, and interviewers. What great firsthand experience! I remember the time when I took one of my male students, Roshaun, to interview Tia and Tamara Mowry. The twins were big Hollywood stars in the midst of their successful TV show, *Sister Sister*. We were interviewing them because they were committed Christians, and their agent granted us a half-hour interview before they spoke at a local church. Roshaun did an amazing job conducting the interview, and we managed to come away with a very nice story, despite his being star-struck and extremely excited. (I was pretty excited, too, I must admit.)

I returned to the Biola Christian Writers Conference in 1992, and this time another editor said again that I had a good start with my Bible-study-turned-book. However, one publisher from a very large publishing house actually took my proposal and sample chapters back to his company. Over the next few months, readers reviewed my work and I rewrote it again. Finally, I received a call from the company. The person on the phone said they enjoyed my idea, but they were going in a different direction. She asked, "Could you turn this into a Bible study?" How ironic!

The book had started out as a Bible study and had grown into a book I was proud of, so I decided to self-publish the work instead.

Now with the magazine *Christteen*, my first article published in another magazine, and my self-published book, *Me? Virtuous?*, I was officially a freelance writer—an official authorpreneur.

During that '92 conference, I sat at one lunch table with Marita Littauer. She asked me why I had come, and when I said I was an author, she countered, "Well if you're an author, you will have to become a speaker."

"How do I do that?" I asked.

Marita introduced me to CLASS Speakers Service. Marita's mother was Florence Littauer, a well-known author and motivational speaker, who had started CLASS, "Christian Leaders, Authors, and Speakers Services." CLASS existed to teach Christian professionals to speak. A three-day CLASS seminar was coming up at the Biola location in just a few weeks, so I decided to attend.

At the end of the conference, the closing event speaker challenged us to write our short and long-term goals. We made two copies: one we kept, the other we turned in. The conference faculty divided up these goal sheets and committed to pray for the people whose sheets they got. Six months after the conference, I was pretty excited to receive a letter from the faculty member who had received my list.

She was an author whose books I had read, and was writing to say she was still praying for me and to see how I was getting along with my goals. We struck up a friendship and kept in touch. Knowing of my teaching career (and by then I had attended my first CLASS seminar) and my growing writing talent, she invited me to teach at a small, local writers' conference.

I also attended the 1992 Mount Hermon Christian Writers Conference near San Jose, California, for the first time. The Mount Hermon conference was the first writers' conference established in the country, so it's considered the granddaddy of them all. And indeed that is true. For many years, Mount Hermon boasted the largest and most influential faculty, and offered workshops for beginning, middle, and advanced writers. Attendees returned year after year, not only for the benefit of furthering their writing careers, but also for the fellowship with fellow writers. I was hooked from the first year I attended.

Interestingly, I was the only African-American among several hundred attendees. I told conference director David Talbot that I was managing editor of *Christteen* magazine, and although I wasn't officially on the faculty for the event, I could take appointments and possibly publish some of the attendees' work. To introduce me to the conferees, David interviewed me during one of the meals, but besides just talking about *Christteen*, he ventured off script and asked my opinion concerning how to get more people of color to attend the conference. I answered, "Put me on staff." The conferees burst into applause, and God has made it possible for me to be on the Mount Hermon faculty every year except one ever since.

That year at Mount Hermon, I also met Gayle Roper, who was the director of the Sandy Cove Christian Writers Conference held in Northeast, Maryland. Her faculty was full, but if I could get there, she would allow me to represent *Christteen* with the promise of putting me on her staff the following year. I didn't have the money to pay for a ticket to fly across the country, but a woman who had overheard our conversation offered to pay for my trip, so in October, off I went to Sandy Cove. I became a fixture there as well, moving from faculty member, to assistant director, and then to director until the conference center decided not to host a writers' conference any longer.

During the rest of the 1990s, I continued editing *Christteen* and became more established as the published author of many magazine articles in other publications and pieces in collection books. I also received an assignment to write a book for hire for Scandinavia Publishing House. The book, *Dr. Martin Luther King, Jr.: The Pastor Who Had a Daring*

Dream, was published in Norwegian. It's pretty funny that it is my first traditionally published book, and I can't even read it!

Through those years, due to situations unrelated to my writing, my marriage was deteriorating. The stress caused my health to take a hit, too. I suffered a collapsed lung and needed care that I had to get from public, outpatient services because my soon-to-be ex-husband stopped working and lost our health insurance. Still, my walk with the Lord became closer as I experienced this extremely difficult time.

Even though I had published a book on being a virtuous woman whose husband would "have no need of spoil" and "rise and call [me] blessed," my marriage ended in May of 1999. My situation conformed clearly to the Biblical exceptions, but I had never imagined I would be divorced, and regrettably found myself bankrupt, displaced from my home thanks to repossession, and a single mom with full custody of my two young sons.

The years 1999 to early 2001 were hard, but God carried me through them. The boys and I moved several times, but always to better and better locations until I was a homeowner again. Despite the losses, I was blessed. My job at South Bay Lutheran High School remained constant, as did the love of my extended family and friends, the health and successes of my boys, and my writing and speaking that was becoming a business and ministry.

Don't get me wrong—I made some mistakes during this time, the largest of which was hooking back up with an ex-boyfriend. This rebound relationship left me feeling like I had messed up so badly that God could no longer use me. However, I had one more speaking engagement on my calendar, so I made another deal with God. I said, "God, these women don't deserve for me to cancel on them. Please take me across country and minister to them through me. I know my mistakes have made me unqualified for You to use me any further after that, but please anoint me just this once more. From then on, I'll sit in the pew and quietly worship You."

Just as God had supplied my desire to give back to writers by teaching at writers conferences, God showed me that He loved me, and told me (through one of the other speakers) He wasn't finished using me as a writer and speaker regardless of sinful inadequacies. Guess what? All God has to use are people with sinful inadequacies. He's forgiven us and expects us to use those very inadequacies to minister to others the truth of their possibilities.

On March 8, 2001, I went on my first date with a wonderful man, and on August 4 of that same year, we were married. *Christteen* had gone out of business a few years earlier, but I was established as a freelance writer by then, so I continued fulfilling invitations to teach at writers' conferences across the country, and I was receiving more and more invitations to speak and keynote at conventions, retreats, services, teas, and luncheons.

In 2003, my new husband, James, financed the publishing of my first teen title, *What? Teenagers in the Bible?*, currently in its second printing, now from Redemption Press. Since then the number of my published books has risen to ten. There are two more women's books, two parenting books, a prayer devotional, a term paper handbook, and the latest, a children's book, is the first in a planned seven-book series.

For me, being an authorpreneur has meant going through the doors God opens. Presently, Life That Matters Ministries is the umbrella ministry that houses the five branches of the business to which God has called me, including writing devotionals, leading seminars and editorial consulting (AuthorizeMe®), organizing spa retreats for Christian women (Milk & Honey Life Retreats), writing books, and speaking.[1] I am the editor-in-chief of *Gospel Roads* magazine, an online publication, and the hostess of the Internet TV show "Life That Matters with Sharon Norris Elliott."[2]

My website, YouTube channel, Facebook, Twitter, and LinkedIn accounts are just scratching the surface of social media. I'm also now licensed in ministry and have enrolled at Golden Gate Baptist Theological Seminary to pursue my master's degree.

Twenty-four years in this business. It's been amazing, moving from knowing nothing about the Christian publishing industry to being a real part of it. I have a long, long way to go, just as I would if I were twenty-four years old again. There are lots more books in my head, and I'm confident that God has more ideas yet to give me.

The authorpreneur life continues.

W. Terry Whalin, a writer and acquisitions editor at Morgan James Publishing, lives in Colorado. A former magazine editor and literary agent, he has also written more than sixty nonfiction books including his newest, *Jumpstart Your Publishing Dreams* and *Billy Graham*.

To help writers (fiction and nonfiction), he has created a twelve-lesson online course called "Write A Book Proposal." Check out his free e-book, *Platform Building Ideas for Every Author*.

Contact him at TerryWhalin.com and on Twitter @TerryWhalin, at Facebook.com/TerryWhalin, and at LinkedIn.com/in/TerryWhalin.

CHAPTER FIVE

ALWAYS LEARNING

W. Terry Whalin

The world of book publishing is ever-changing. What was effective five years ago to reach readers is different today.

But these changes aren't new. I encourage you to locate and read former Simon and Schuster Editor-in-Chief Michael Korda's *Making the List, A Cultural History of the American Bestseller 1900-1999.*[1] Publishers, editors, and agents are—and have always been—trying to pick books and authors which will sell enough copies to make the bestseller list.

> The bestseller list is full of surprises, too [Korda writes]. Publishers have always bemoaned the fate of the dreaded "first novel," but the bestseller lists are full of first novels by unknown authors that sold hundreds

of thousands of copies—even millions of copies—and made their author, and publisher, rich and famous. Margaret Mitchell's *Gone With the Wind* is the example that comes to everybody's mind. (p. xiii)

A little later, Korda says, "Editors cling to the advice that's always worked for them, when dealing with authors— 'Concentrate on story, story, story!' 'Show, don't tell!'" (p. xxv)

Now as an acquisitions editor, authors often want me to predict whether their book will be a bestseller.[2] While I can recognize a well-written book, I learned years ago it is unwise to predict which books will bomb and which will become bestsellers.

As we tell our Morgan James authors, *every bookstore* buys books based on their perception of what the author is going to be doing to promote the book. We have a system established to regularly take the reports from our authors and feed them to the bookstores in order to keep our books selling in the stores. I recommend every author find out how to report their regular activity to their publisher.

My personal watershed moment as an author came at Mega Book Marketing University in 2007. I attended as a literary agent and listened carefully to each session. I had written over fifty-five books with traditional publishers, yet I was doing almost nothing to promote my books. Yes, I had a personal website,[3] but I had no teleseminars,[4] a few entries in my blog[5] and no Twitter followers.[6] I decided to change and take action. I became actively involved in the promotion of my books and building an audience of readers with a newsletter[7] and regular communication. I would not delegate or outsource this activity to a designer or a webmaster, but I did it myself. I've built a large digital footprint—and here's the good news: you can do it too.

Every author is surrounded with opportunity (even if you don't know it). The activities to build an audience don't have to consume your life or prevent your writing—but you do need to take consistent action. I am constantly learning about publishing, bookselling, and marketing. There is *always* more to learn, and I will never figure it all out. And that's okay.

Here are nine principles I've learned as I've engaged the market (which I've expanded in *Jumpstart Your Publishing Dreams*[8]):

1. Always be prepared.
2. Decide to be consistent.
3. Decide to be generous and help others.
4. Count the cost of new activities.
5. Gain knowledge before you leap into an activity.
6. Look for ways to automate.
7. Be open to new tools.
8. Don't neglect old fashion print tools.
9. Create a clear goal for each new tool.

I wish I could say that I have it all figured out—but I don't. I'm still growing in my daily knowledge of this publishing business. But I wouldn't have it any other way, because I have chosen to follow my passion for the printed page every day.

I know books change lives, because many years ago, reading a book changed *my* life.[9]

Tyora Moody is the author of "soul-searching suspense" novels in the Serena Manchester Series, Victory Gospel Series, and the Eugeena Patterson Mysteries. As a literary-focused entrepreneur, she has assisted countless authors with developing an online presence via her design and marketing company, Tywebbin Creations, LLC; popular services include virtual event planning, social media management, book trailers, and book covers.

She is also the author of the nonfiction series *The Literary Entrepreneur's Toolkit*, and the host of *The Literary Entrepreneur Podcast*.

For more information about her literary endeavors, visit her online at TyoraMoody.com.

CHAPTER SIX

THE LITERARY ENTREPRENEUR'S JOURNEY BEGINS NOW

Tyora Moody

If you are a new author, congratulations on your recent or upcoming book release. Are you hoping to achieve bestseller status? You certainly can, but with a bit more effort than you originally thought. Just in case no one told you, publishing a book is a phenomenal achievement, but there's this other element lurking around the corner…

That's right—you have to tell people about the book! It's called book marketing. So, in reality, you're more than an author—you are a literary entrepreneur. Writing and marketing books is a business.

I've been working with authors since 1999—both traditional and self-published. In 2010, I personally crossed over to being an author, so, as an already established entrepreneur, I've seen two sides to building an online presence, for clients and for myself.

I think it's very important when it comes to book marketing that we think like a reader. It's so easy to fall into the author mode where all we want is for someone to purchase our book and read our story. Believe me, I know.

Books have been a part of my life since I was a little girl. Relatives knew to give me books as gifts for birthdays and Christmas. I hung out at the library at least once a week, spending hours between dusty shelves. When I was old enough to make my own money, I grew to love bookstores. I'm a female who doesn't care for shopping, but I will spend hard-earned money on books. Quite the handy-woman, I have also assembled quite a few bookshelves of my own over the years, too.

I have always loved holding a book in my hand. When e-books started becoming popular, I was one of those people balking at the idea of not being able to hold a real, actual book. A few years ago, I made my first trip from the east coast to California. I wanted to travel light, and I really didn't want to carry too many items in my carry-on suitcase. I decided to download the Kindle app to my iPhone; the first book I purchased was from one of my favorite suspense authors. By the time I returned home, I had read an almost-300-page book on the Kindle app. I was stunned.

Needless to say, I purchased my first Kindle a few weeks later. Now I still have my books and bookcases, but traveling with the Kindle versus a stack of books was a huge deal for me.

I share this story mainly because e-books literally have changed the face of publishing and the way readers consume books. The shift also has allowed more people to jump into the self-publishing business, thus making book marketing even more important. Being creative and unique in this business is what's going to determine how many readers you can attract to your books. *Think like a reader!*

Have you ever found yourself saying, "I can't do this online stuff," or "I'm not computer literate," or "I'm too old for this," or "This is too much work"? If you are a person who tends to stay on the excuse-side, then you may be disappointed. I'm not giving you get-rich-quick tips, nor am I'm guaranteeing you are going to be on *The New York Times* bestselling list in a month.

I became an entrepreneur before the thought ever entered my mind; I like to tell people my business found me. My first author client came knocking when I was creating websites as a hobby. When the door opened to build websites, I walked through that door and over a decade later have worked with countless authors. That's years of late nights after coming home from the day job and many sacrificed weekends of learning the craft, keeping up with the changing industry, keeping loyal clients satisfied, and attracting new clients.

I grew up with workaholics, and I've accepted that I am one as an adult. I love technology and have always had a deep desire to know the nuts and bolts of how something works. Once I know how it works, that's when the creativity and fun starts.

So, are you open-minded?

I have to ask this question because the same creative effort you put into writing a book is the same one you need in order to be open-minded enough to strategize and implement creative ways to market your books.

Before I received my first book contract, I had a PR friend tell me I needed to think about marketing long before the book hits the shelves. Marketing should be on your mind *as you're writing the book.* Now you might be reading this and thinking, *How I can concentrate on writing and book marketing at the same time?* Believe me, that concept seems overwhelming to digest, but it can be done.

Though I'm focusing on online marketing at the moment, I would be remiss not to mention that to successfully promote a book, you need a balance of offline and online book publicity. You can't solely concentrate on one. I can tell you there's nothing quite like face to face interaction with a reader. What is even more amazing is when you meet a reader who you have connected with on social media. That name and avatar is standing in front of you as a real person with a copy of your book, and they want your autograph. This is where relationship building is important.

The days of getting by without an online presence are over—you know that, right? Whether you are a traditionally published or self-published author, daydreaming about your bestseller will not sell a single book. As soon as you have a release date, it's time to get down to the *business* of book marketing, preferably six to nine months in advance.

Now I know you're probably like many other authors, who don't have a tremendous amount of free time to devote to book marketing. There are the nine-to-five jobs, raising your family, taking care of elderly parents, and/or community activities. Even if there is an opportunity to write fulltime, some authors still have to supplement their income by providing services like editing, teaching, or speaking. With all of this going on in your life, no wonder book marketing makes you cringe.

Authors, how you approach book marketing is critical. There's no need to release a book if you don't get this. You're more than an author—you're a literary entrepreneur. You are in the business of writing. You're in the business that many large publishers have been doing for years. This is *big* business. Look at Amazon. Love or hate them—big business: they do it well.

You can market well, too!

Marketing starts with understanding your target audience. This is the first essential step in any kind of marketing. Do you write fiction or nonfiction? If you write fiction, which genre—romance, suspense, fantasy? If you write nonfiction, is your book a memoir or self-help?

It helps to define early on who the target audience or reader is who most likely will be interested in your book.

Most book marketers agree it's easier to develop a platform for nonfiction books than fiction books. Oftentimes a nonfiction writer has a niche audience that is seeking information, which can be provided online via a blog or webinars. If a nonfiction writer has strong speaking skills, he or she can develop a pretty robust speaking platform where they can market books.

Before I wrote my first nonfiction book, I had completed four novels, so I have been concentrated on marketing fiction for a while. I can tell you the audience for my fiction and nonfiction is different, although there may be some crossover for readers who are aspiring writers or authors. The marketing plans, though, were certainly not the same.

I knew when I started writing my first novel in 2006 that my focus would be on readers who like mystery or suspense in a Christian-based novel. I also knew my core audience would probably be women between the ages of twenty-five to fifty-five. You might be asking how I knew that much detail. These details came from a combination of learning to understand my characters, and research of similar published novels on the shelf.

Many authors who write fiction spend quite a bit of time creating character profiles or sketches. Those profiles help with character development, but also may prove to be helpful later when thinking about your readership. I'm not supporting being a cookie-cutter writer, but you should be aware of what sells.

When I first started writing my novel, I wrote what I considered to be a suspense novel. After a few author friends read my first manuscript, they encouraged me to consider adding romantic elements to the novel if I wanted to appeal more to the demographics I was seeking. Romance is the number one bestselling genre in fiction, and women tend to buy a lot more books. Keeping that in mind, I restructured my novel to include both a female and male point-of-view, and my romantic suspense series was born.

While I don't like comparisons, they are important and vital to understanding your target audience. If you work with a traditional publisher, they will want you to include novels for comparison in your marketing plans. You can start this process by searching on Amazon. Ask yourself the following questions:

- What other authors share the readership that you're looking for to purchase your books?

- What can you do different to appeal to those readers and keep your stories unique?

- If you're self-published and you're considering your book packaging, how can you make sure you have a book cover that equals the quality of a traditionally published book in the same genre?

Also, think about marketing as you write. Don't concentrate so hard on the finished product without thinking about the bigger picture. There are certain issues or situations in a book that you could pull out in your marketing. For example:

- *Can the media call you?* During the research phase of your book, you may have gained a vast knowledge on a subject and could prove yourself to be a resource. Do you already have the education or experience credentials? What type of news event can you pitch as an expert to a local television station, radio station, newspaper, or magazine? Do not diss the local media around you. Everyone has to start somewhere and work their way to larger media markets.

- *Can you contribute to a special event or cause?* There are many events that provide opportunities to speak or contribute throughout the year. Do you have a character in your fiction book with relatable issues? For example, if you have a character suffering from breast cancer, you may want to keep October in mind since its Breast Cancer Awareness Month. Research a calendar of events and observance themes.

- *Do you have a topic that you can expand beyond the book?* Why not approach leaders or members of an organization as a possible speaker or expert? Pitch an article or blog post to a magazine or website? Do you have enough material to develop a workshop, seminar, or webinar? Can you launch an event or sponsor a conference? Think *big* and strategic!

These opportunities and more can help build a platform, which is essential for marketing. Any opportunities to position your author brand can increase your chances of growing your readership. The earlier you're aware of opportunities, the earlier you will start contacting and assembling the necessary elements to launch your book marketing plan.

Here are five book marketing tips I want to leave you with for your journey. Think of them as a quick checklist for any new book release.

1. *Start early!* While you are writing the book, marketing should be considered. What are some themes or current issues that generate discussion or attract the media? Keep a notebook of ideas. As you draw closer to your release, use an editorial calendar so you are aware of special events, holidays, etc.

2. *Create a website.* Create a website first, then social media profiles and pages. Your professional website is the hub of your online presence. It's the one central location (that you own) where you can keep a downloadable media kit and free excerpts, or send readers to sign up for your mailing list.

3. *Join social networks.* When you spend time building relationships using social media platforms, you have the potential to attract a readership or influencers for your book. Remember, the best form of advertisement is word of mouth. Now don't overwhelm yourself. Start with two. Or even one. Study the best times to post and be creative.

4. *Seek book reviews.* Family and friends are nice, but build teams of support by connecting with book bloggers and reviewers. Be sure to have review copies or galleys at least three to six months before book release, both e-book and hard copies.

5. *Market your book consistently.* I want to encourage you to spend anywhere from ten to thirty minutes each day on book marketing. You can use this time to brainstorm new ideas and evaluate what did or didn't work. As an offline example, you can use the time to hand out postcards or bookmarks at an event. Or spend quality time online scheduling posts or tweets to social networks. Stay consistent with your book marketing.

You can do it!

Rochelle Carter is the Publisher at Ellechor Media LLC, an award-winning publishing company with three imprints and an online bookstore. She provides premium self-publishing services, training, and coaching for authors, and manages the acquisition and production process for her traditional imprint.

Carter has received national recognition for her leadership and professional achievements, including the 2014 Stiletto Woman in Business Award for Entrepreneur of the Year and as a runner-up for the 2015 Portland Business Journal's Forty Under 40 list.

As the international bestselling author of the 2014 USA Best Book Award Winner, *The 7-Step Guide to Authorpreneurship*, *Becoming An Author*, *Write Success*, and *Christian Authorpreneurship: Mastering the Business of Publishing*, Rochelle Carter is dedicated to creating "Independent, Innovative, and Iconic twenty-first century authors."

Contact her at RochelleCarter.com, on Twitter @RochelleDCarter and on Facebook at Facebook.com/Ellechor

CHAPTER SEVEN

AUTHORPRENEURSHIP UNLEASHED

Rochelle Carter

Authorpreneurs are leaders. They don't take "no" or "I can't afford it" as viable answers, and they are strategic in their movements. They are human, so they make mistakes like the rest of us, but in the end, they are still pushing forward and finding ways to maximize on their mistakes to keep pushing toward the mark.

I never set out to be an authorpreneur. In fact, I had enough of a long history of incomplete stories and novels to have decided at a young age that I would never be an author. Luckily this decision did not dull my love for reading or my motivation to add my own unique legacy to the world.

BECOMING AN ENTREPRENEUR

I was (and still am) a Human Resources Project Manager. My key functionality involved analyzing business processes and systems, making recommendations, and leading projects to help the business become more efficient. I have over ten years of experience, and yet I did not love my *job*; I loved helping people. I loved the idea of creating something new for the business, but my job and I had a casual relationship that, for a time, I felt was good enough.

When the economy started crashing and those around me started losing their jobs, however, I had to wonder if it really was good enough. What stability did I have? Why was I breaking my neck each day if, in the end, "corporate" wouldn't hesitate to axe my peers or even me so they could maintain large profit margins?

It was time for a change, but I did not know where to begin. I was still working fulltime, so when would I even be able to think about options?

Authorpreneurs always find a way, some way, somehow.

I have always been an avid reader and a writer, but when I considered life in publishing after reading a particularly terrible book, a small voice inside of me told me I should monetize my skills as a publisher instead. While I loved writing, reading, and learning about authorship, I was much more confident in my organization and project management skills. I decided in that moment to become an entrepreneur-while-working. I quickly determined that my first priority was to "do publishing right," and that I would also learn what that meant!

I named my company Ellechor Media, LLC (dba Ellechor Publishing House, LLC). Using my project management skills and knowing that the best person for any specialized job is a subject-matter expert, I found my team of professional publishers, designers, editors, and marketing specialists. I then sought out contract professionals to help me put together our business plan, create an awesome website, and put out our first official call for submissions. We found our first authors almost immediately. I was ready to go, and this was the perfect timing because my life was stable enough to support a business…

Or so I thought!

I made Ellechor wait a full year before starting to release any books, hoping to get a good head start on the process, vet the appropriate contractors, and have time to edit, re-edit, and proof everything.

The best-laid plans don't factor in real life.

I ended up with severe preeclampsia in the hospital just six months into my first pregnancy and four months before our first three books launched. This was where having a reliable "Power Team" paid off. With me out of commission, my team carried on with my plans to launch our first books and manage our preparation for the next season of book releases. I was now officially an entrepreneur with products available to the public.

Going through the early years of the business had its difficulties, but in the end, it continues to be a life-changing experience. We have won various awards and nominations;

I learned a lot; I continue to learn; and I am always seeking ways to share with others.

As my author list grew, however, I quickly discovered that authors did not just need their books published. While that is his or her immediate goal, the true necessary tool for *every* author is knowledge—knowledge about the publishing process, the industry, and how to navigate those confusing waters.

BECOMING AN *AUTHOR*PRENEUR

I am a publisher. I have over ten years of project management experience and six years of experience in book publishing, and I *love my job*. I love helping authors take their work from a manuscript to a physical, tangible book they can hug and love. In building Ellechor Publishing House, I was building a legacy that I hope will endure for a long time.

And yet I still felt there was something missing. My authors, while happy to be published, had so many questions about the business that at one point I was spending hours a day just answering emails. It took me a while, but it finally hit me: despite there being so much information available on publishing a book, there was still a missing component.

I went looking for a resource I could recommend to new authors to help them understand the business side of writing, but what I found was disappointing. Every book had its own agenda, focusing on writing, marketing, and the basics of self-publishing or becoming a fulltime publisher. Many consisted of what could be called blog posts without any real value within their pages. What my authors needed, and what many other authors need as well, is a book that takes them through the *entire* process of publishing a book from the author perspective.

Authorpreneurs see a need and are committed to filling it, providing value for the reader.

I had to be the one to make it happen, because if not me, then who? I knew exactly what I wanted my authors to know, the questions they were asking, and the struggle they faced without a one-on-one coach to hand hold them every step of the way. One year later I released my bestselling book, *The 7-Step Guide to Authorpreneurship* (June 24, 2014, EverFaith Press), which educates writers on how to understand the business of writing and become successful authors.

The same month I was awarded the 2014 Stiletto Woman in Business Entrepreneur of the Year Award, and I became the first African-American woman whose book won the 2014 USA Best Book Award Winner in Business: Writing & Publishing.

Writing *The 7-Step Guide to Authorpreneurship* was just the beginning for me. I am taking the book further by developing online training for authors who want hands-on experience with the steps in my book. With the launch of my Brand Your Expertise with a Book™ program[1] and

The Authorpreneurship Project,[2] I will continue to focus on educating authors on the business of writing, providing the tools and resources they need to become "Independent, Innovative, and Iconic twenty-first century authors." This work, in addition to book packaging for aspiring authorpreneurs with my self-publishing imprint at Ellechor Media, has me in my professional sweet spot, and I love every minute of it!

You know you are doing the right thing when despite things falling apart they also seem to pull things together. It's a challenge I have accepted, along with higher accountability to my authors and publishing team. I am not perfect, but I will always get back up again and try harder. As I journey into the world of author education, I realize that God is pushing me in this direction so that everything I do can revolve around the things I love and cherish. In wearing my own shoes, I am not just taking the easy street. Rather, I am living, learning, and growing in what I am passionate about and what I believe I was called to do.

Nina Amir, the bestselling author of *How to Blog a Book* and *The Author Training Manual*, is a speaker, a blogger, and an author, book, and blog-to-book coach. Known as the "Inspiration to Creation Coach," she helps creative people combine their passion and purpose so they move from idea to inspired action and positively and meaningfully impact the world as writers, bloggers, authorpreneurs, and blogpreneurs.

Some of Nina's clients have sold 300,000-plus copies of their books, landed deals with major publishing houses, and created thriving businesses around their books. She is the founder of National Nonfiction Writing Month, aka the Write Nonfiction in November Challenge, and the Nonfiction Writers' University. As a hybrid author, she has published fifteen books and had as many as four books on the Amazon Top 100 list at the same time.

Contact her on her website at NinaAmir.com.

CHAPTER EIGHT
FROM INSPIRATION TO CREATION

Nina Amir

When I began my journey to become an author, I never considered becoming an authorpreneur. Now, I work with aspiring authors and always recommend they consider ways to build a business around their books.

It's easy to feel consumed with a book idea and to miss the opportunities to leverage that content into multiple streams of income. Not only that, most writers wear blinders; they only see the book in front of them. They don't see the greater vision of who they can become as an author, which includes additional book ideas and the products and services they can create to go with each one.

MY BEGINNINGS

I started writing when I was in elementary school. I began with stories about horses. I believe even then writing was my passion, and I know writing is my life purpose.

In high school I got involved in writing-related activities. I revived the high school newspaper, which was defunct, and I wrote a biweekly school column for the local newspaper. I wrote a journal for many years, and I dreamed of becoming a novelist. But my mother told me, "Only a good writer can create a career as a novelist." I took that to mean that I wasn't a good enough writer to become a novelist and should find some different type of writing career.

So I took a journalism class in high school; the teacher was charismatic, and I always liked magazines, especially self-help magazines. I decided I would become a magazine journalist, and that is how I set out on my career path.

I attended Syracuse University to get a degree in magazine journalism, where we received a broad education that included newspaper writing, design, and photography. I graduated and worked as an editor for several regional magazines and as an associate editor in the employee communications for a corporation. After that I took a job as an editor for a consultant and managed four newsletters. Later, I started my own business doing freelance newsletters and article writing, working with ad agencies, and a variety of other odd writing-related jobs.

Then, a friend came to me and said, "Can you edit a book?"

My college professor had told us that, as magazine journalists, we could also become authors because a nonfiction book consists of a string of articles on the same topic. I thought, *Well, I've edited magazines and magazine articles, and I've written magazine articles, so I must be able to edit a book, even if I haven't written one.* I agreed to do the job.

I edited that book, and the author recommended me to another person who was a partner in a consultancy. They self-published *Enlightened Leadership*, then submitted it to Simon and Schuster. Simon and Schuster picked up the book verbatim, and it has been in print for approximately twenty years now with their Fireside imprint. *Enlightened Leadership* has sold well over 300,000 copies. That was a big success for me.

A year or two later, I edited a manuscript for a real estate agent who wanted to become an author and develop a business around his book. He self-published *Radical Forgiveness*, then submitted it to the Writers' Digest Awards for self-published titles. That year he won in the inspirational category and got a huge advance and a deal with a traditional publishing company. Unfortunately, the publisher was purchased by a larger company, and his book got put on hold. He was already selling tons of copies, though; so he bought it back and went on to sell over 150,000 copies before he sold it to Sounds True many years later.

Not only was *Radical Forgiveness* another one of my big success stories, but the author, Colin Tipping, also demonstrated to me how one might build a business around a book. He went on to become quite successful with a website, webinars, live events, and more books.

BECOMING AN AUTHOR

I went on to edit quite a number of other books, and I started to pursue my own career as an author. Working with other authors and editing their books made me want to write my own. I began to research how to get published and become a successful author—research that would later become one of my areas of expertise.

I wanted to write books about what I call "practical spirituality" and personal development. I was quite involved in personal development—taking courses on personal growth, motivation, relationships, metaphysics, spirituality, manifestation, and those sorts of things. I'm passionate about these topics.

In conjunction with my desire to write books, I also had a desire to become a speaker and enter what we now call "the expert industry." I wanted to write, speak, and provide online and live courses, much like my former client Colin Tipping.

I quickly learned that I needed an "author platform," or built-in readership for my books. Otherwise, I might not be able to interest a traditional publisher or self-publish successfully. The Internet provided me with numerous ways to get my message read by my target market, including blogging. I started my first blog back in 2006 and a second blog in 2007. I had five blogs at one point—I now have four—but they provided me with a way to be visible, or discoverable, to develop some fans and followers, and to begin my path as an author.

My first book idea involved the Jewish Sabbath (Shabbat) and candle lighting. I produced a book proposal, which I sent out and received some good feedback on from a few literary agents and publishers. But I didn't have a platform.

I often tell the story about when I sent out that very first proposal. One particular literary agent called me. "We love your book idea," she said, "and we love the title. We love your writing, and you wrote a super proposal. But we can't publish you because you have no platform. Nobody knows who you are."

She sent me off to contact a small publishing house. I wanted a big publishing house, but I contacted them anyway. The publisher called me and said, "I've been waiting for this book forever!" We had a forty-five-minute conversation. Then he didn't publish the book either—even though he complimented me, compared me with one of his best writers, and loved the concept!

I then realized it wasn't so easy to become a published author and that I needed to do much more than produce a good book idea and a well-written manuscript. That's when I truly ventured into authorpreneurship, which to me involves building a business around your book.

DO MORE THAN WRITE

In 2007, I ran a virtual class several times on Shabbat candle lighting. It involved four teleseminars based on the book I wanted to write. Then I turned my notes for the class into a short e-book on the subject. I still sell that book, *The Priestess Practice*, today as a PDF from my website.

I found a literary agent around 2006, and we tried selling that book, but we didn't find a publisher to take it on. I switched literary agencies in 2008, and my new agent tried to sell another book I had written about Jewish mysticism. The market was changing, though, and she recommended I write what she called "business books"—really books about publishing nonfiction—because that now was my area of expertise.

By this time I had gained quite a bit of knowledge about how to get published because I was so intent on doing so. I had started the Write Nonfiction in November challenge, and I was involved with the San Francisco Writers Conference. I also possessed personal knowledge of writing for magazines and about writing and publishing a book.

My agent was peddling a proposal based on a book idea that would later become *The Author Training Manual* when I had the idea for *How to Blog a Book*. I wrote *How to Blog a Book* on my blog by the same name, and it received a contract from Writers' Digest Books in 2011. It was published in 2012; it immediately became an Amazon bestseller—and has remained one ever since. (The second edition will be released in June.)

AUTHOR AND AUTHORPRENEUR

In the process of writing and publishing that book, I started to create a few small products to go with it upon its release. My first product was truly an MVP (minimum viable product)—a teleseminar recording about how to blog a book. I then created a short and primitive audio course about on the same topic.

In 2013, authorpreneurship became as large a focus for me as writing books. I started conducting more teleseminars and webinars, and I created the Author of Change Transformational Coaching Program, a three-month-long program with webinars, handouts, and extra mini-programs that included e-books and workbooks.

With this program under my belt, I threw myself into product creation. The next year I created another course, "Author Training 101: How to Craft Books That Sell." I wrote the manuscript for my next book, *The Author Training Manual*, during the eight-week program. The first draft of the book became the course text for my students; they served as my beta readers! I had created a course and written a book at the same time. I already had a contract for the book with Writers' Digest Books, and it was released in March of 2014.

Since then I have gotten more involved in product creation.

I created a how-to-blog-a-book course for the Writers' Digest University (WDU), and I just produced a new program for WDU about crafting a business plan for your book and career. I offer a variety of editing, writing, coaching, and consulting services, plus I have a large number of products including a proposal template, a membership site (the

Nonfiction Writers' University), additional courses, and a variety of e-books. All of these help me get my message and my content to my potential readers—people who can use the information to improve their lives and their careers. Building a business around my book—becoming an authorpreneur—helps me be of service to the people who needed this information. That's the key: to provide your potential readers what they need and want, to answer their questions, to provide solutions to their problems, to ease their pain.

TWO TIPS ON HOW TO GET STARTED

If I could offer two bits of advice to aspiring authors and authorpreneurs, the first would be to *have a vision of your destination* and plan how you will get there. In other words, know what success looks like to you, think ahead as you plan your career, and set goals that help you take steps toward reaching your destination.

I still want to write those books about personal development and practical spirituality. However, I didn't have a big-picture view of my career when I first started, and how to reach my destination—successful authorship. I didn't plan how to become an authorpreneur or a member of the expert industry. Because of that, I took a more winding road than necessary.

In fact, after creating willy-nilly rather than according to a plan, I had to do quite a bit of work to brand my company and myself. It took me about a year to figure out how to bring all my interests and projects together under one umbrella brand—Nina Amir, the Inspiration to Creation Coach.

However, I still have a long way to go. I have a list of twelve books yet to write, each one with the potential for products and services. By moving from one project to the next, eventually I will get from where I am now to where I want to be. Where is that? It's a place (or a time) when I can write books and provide services that combine my expertise in writing and publishing nonfiction and blogging and blogging books with my passion and interest in spirituality and personal development. I want to help people "**A**chieve **M**ore **I**nspired **R**esults" and to fulfil their purpose and potential—and I hope to do that with my books and the businesses I build around them.

I feel pushed all the time to write more, yet there are so many other things to do, product creation being an important one of them. Becoming an authorpreneur is how you support yourself as a writer and author. Most authors can't earn a living only with money earned from royalties. If you don't want to take on another job so you can keep writing, focus on monetizing your content. At least then your business revolves around your writing.

My second bit of advice to those wanting to build a business around their books is to *start with a small and manageable project*. Many writers are put off by technology. Technology can be daunting, so start simply. Do a free teleseminar on some aspect of your book. Sell the recording along with a transcript of the event (this becomes your first product). Or produce a workbook or an audio or email course based upon your book. These products can be produced quite simply. (Get more information on how to do so in *Authorpreneur: How to Build a Business Around Your Book.*[1])

When I look at my body of work—traditionally published books, self-published e-books, blogs, products, and services—one thing becomes clear to me: My biggest success lies in the fact that I can reach so many people with my message and help them in some way. When I get an email from somebody who says, "This course [or blog post, audio, teleseminar, webinar, etc.] was exactly what I needed today," or "Your book changed my life! It inspired me to start writing," that's better than a ten thousand dollar check. That is why I do what I do.

I am an authorpreneur because I want to inspire people to share their positive and meaningful messages with the world, to make a difference, and to live the lives they want to live. Producing more than just books gives me more opportunities to help my readers fulfill their potential and purpose. That allows me to fulfill mine.

Tom Blubaugh was raised in a small town in southeast Kansas. He began writing poetry at age fourteen, but has written nonfiction most of his adult life. He self-published his first book, *Behind the Scenes of the Bus Ministry*, in 1974, and wrote articles for denominational and business magazines from 1975 through 1995. He cowrote *The Great Adventure* for Barbour Publishing Co. in 2009. Bound by Faith Publishers published his first novel, *Night of the Cossack*, in April, 2011, when he was 69.

Tom has been a public speaker for over forty years, and is currently a Literary Strategist working one-on-one with authors and writers in all aspects of the publishing arena, social media, brand building, and book marketing. Tom has been a self-employed entrepreneur since 1973, and is married to Barbara; they have six children and fourteen grandchildren.

Find out more at TomBlubaugh.net.

CHAPTER NINE
TIPS FROM A RUSSIAN WRITING MAVERICK

Tom Blubaugh

When I was fourteen (in 1956), I was too bashful to tell a girl I liked her, so I wrote a poem for her instead. Little did I know this was the beginning of a lifetime of writing.

By the time I had written several poems, Elvis Presley was on the scene. I suddenly envisioned my lyrics becoming songs that Elvis could sing and record. After filling out several applications to publishing companies (comic book ads), I realized they all wanted money. Since I didn't have any, my dream died a painful death.

Fast forward to 1973—I was in Bible College and I had written two term papers on evangelism and drug use in society. I decided to merge the papers into a manuscript for publication to use when I held seminars in churches. With manuscript in hand, I drove to Nashville, Tennessee, to present it to a friend that worked for a denominational publishing house. Three months later, to my horror, I received a letter that my manuscript had been lost—my one and only copy!

For several months I anguished and prayed, and after *a year*, my manuscript showed up in the mail, with a short note stating that the publishing house was not interested in printing my book. Disappointed but determined, I took my manuscript to a local printer and self-published one hundred fifty copies. Although I now had a book with my name on it and I sold all of the copies, I didn't consider myself an author. I did continue to write, though, and had several articles published in business and denominational magazines.

In the early 1980s, I started a children's church in a local congregation. I enlisted a team of women to make puppets, a group of men to build a puppet stage, and a team of people to read and record puppet skits I wrote. For three years I enjoyed seeing children delight in our performances and grow spiritually. Most of my writing for the next twenty years was content writing for websites, financial planning seminars, and family history for my heirs.

In 2005, my mother passed away. I suddenly realized that I only had one relative on my mother's side who was older than I. I had also survived a major heart attack in 2004. These two incidents brought my mortality to the forefront, and I began to think about my legacy.

Both of my grandfathers died before I was born. I didn't have that role model for myself, yet I was a grandfather of fourteen. The thought of leaving something meaningful for them became very important to me, and the idea of writing a story about my maternal grandfather surfaced. He was born a Jew in Russia, was a Cossack soldier, defected, and came to America. This fascinated me, but besides a few other facts, I knew nothing about him.

I interviewed my one living aunt on my mother's side in an attempt to find out as much as I could about my grandfather. Unfortunately, I didn't learn much more than I already knew. Apparently my grandparents spoke seven languages fluently, and when they spoke of the old countries, they spoke in languages their children didn't understand; they wanted their children to be Americans. As a result most of my heritage was lost.

I was determined to leave a heritage for my heirs. Therefore, I took the little bit of information I had, and I began researching the Russian history of the late 1800s and early 1900s. I don't know why I was surprised when the history I researched lined up with the information I had on my family, but it did, which motivated me even more.

After five years I had written a 250-page novel that was historically accurate with a grandfather who was 95 percent fiction. I accomplished this with the encouragement of a published author I met online and a local critique group that was invaluable in helping me in my weakest areas of English and grammar.

Now, how was I going to publish my story?

During this time frame (2009), I was contracted by Barbour Publishing to cowrite a devotional named *The*

Great Adventure. They offered me a deep discount, and I purchased and sold approximately three hundred copies. I was honored, and I began to consider that I might really be an author.

An acquaintance then contacted me and asked me to help him develop a website. He and his wife had decided they wanted to help an author they knew to publish her book. Interestingly enough, I didn't connect this with the possible publication of my own novel.

When I met with them to start the process in 2010, I was showing them some websites I had produced, and shared with them different things that could be done for theirs. One of the sites was my own, on which I had placed a link to the first chapter of my own novel. Later I found out they made a note of the link and read the chapter.

They called me and asked if they could read my manuscript. I agreed, and a short time later, they told me they would like to publish my novel. This started me on a path I hadn't considered seriously; I had only toyed with the idea of publication. My goal was to pass the story down to my heirs, not publish it for others to read. My critique group was encouraging me in that direction, but I hadn't found the submission/rejection process very appealing.

My novel was published in April 2011. This was the time that the publishing industry started into a major change. Amazon had become the biggest bookseller in the world, brick and mortar bookstores were closing down, and publishers were demanding that authors have an established platform before consideration for publication.

Over the next four years, self-publishing started losing the stigma of being second-class or less. Well-established authors began self-publishing their own work because of greater control and higher profits. It was coming down to the point of who was going to pay for publishing the book—the author or publisher? Regardless, the author found that he or she was going to do the lion's share of the marketing.

At the same time, this became probably the most difficult time for someone to start a publishing company. I observed my publishers doing everything they could to get my book into stores, set up book signings and radio interviews, and other marketing strategies. It became very apparent to me that it was as difficult for them to get my book on store shelves as it was for authors to get editors to read their manuscripts.

Consignment-to-store was the only way to get my novel on shelves. This was very difficult for my publishers—not only the bookkeeping, but collecting money from the stores even when they knew books had been sold. I quickly realized that writing the book, even though it took five years, was the easiest part of the publication/marketing process. My publishers had spent several thousands of dollars on cover design, editing, printing, advertising, and other expenses.

By this time I had been in marketing for forty years and self-employed most of that time, but it didn't take me long to realize the book industry was a different ball game. My book was on Amazon and Barnes & Noble's sites, but so were twelve million others. How were people going to find mine?

I personally sold over a thousand copies of my novel. I abused Facebook by using it as an advertising platform to family and friends and anyone else I thought might respond by purchasing a copy. I now know that was the opposite way of building a platform. I was an opera singer singing, "Me, me, me, me."

I researched author groups online, hoping to learn strategies from their members that would help me with my book marketing. What I found, for the most part, were authors who were duplicating what they had seen others do. The problem was that there was no real measurement of the effectiveness and the profitability of these strategies. Attaining the number one spot in a genre of very little competition on Amazon did very little toward helping the author become known.

I began to seriously use social media as a means of building a platform, but it wasn't until I realized the importance of quality over quantity that I made a strong connection with my followers. Developing a brand is more about building relationships than getting my face and my book in front of a huge amount of people. It was time to stop being a salesperson and become a relationship builder, changing the emphasis from selling a product to helping others solve a problem, achieve a goal, or satisfy a need.

Although I had built websites, I began to understand it was outside of my core competencies. There was much more to building a site than putting on a few pictures and writing content. I learned I had only seven seconds to capture a browser's interest, and that they would not purchase until they had seen my book seven times. My site had to offer enough to bring them back six more times.

Over a period of several months, I reinvented myself, combining my years of marketing experience with what I was learning about authors and their needs. I became a Literary Strategist, consulting with authors/writers and developing strategies to help them build a platform. It became my mission to help authors understand that book publishing is a business and has to be treated like such for them to become successful.

At this current time, I have written three books, cowritten two, and guest written in four others. I am working with a significant number of authors/writers who are struggling along the difficult path of publishing and marketing. I speak to author and writing groups including school-age students from the fourth grade to senior high school who have dreams of becoming authors.

An author is a person who writes a novel, poem, essay, or other documents with considerable energy and desire. An entrepreneur is a person who organizes and manages an enterprise, especially a business, with not only energy and desire but risk as well.

Melding the author with the entrepreneur (an author-preneur) is a challenge. It requires a minimum of five attributes:

Willingness

Organization

Reliability

Knowledge

Can you see the fifth attribute? Look very closely at the four words, and four letters will show themselves to you.

That's right—WORK.

It takes an *authorpreneur* to succeed in the world of publishing in the twenty-first century.

Kachelle Kelly is founder of Kachelle Kelly International, Inc., a small business and empowerment coaching firm. Kachelle utilizes her creativity and candor as she coaches career driven women and men to not only activate their hustle but also their faith by providing them with innovative ideas, strategies, resources, and empowerment to achieve authentic success, profitability, peace, and happiness in their business and life.

Her coaching clients rave about her ability to not only understand them and their struggles but also their businesses—knowing exactly how to be "real" in sharing a step-by-step plan to grow their businesses online and offline. Kachelle empowers others to "activate your hustle," encouraging them to actively go after their dreams and visions by eliminating distractions and adopting best business practices to be successful.

She is the author of *Boss Women & Boss Men Pray: 31 Prayers to Increase Your Success & Spirit*, and holds a Bachelor's Degree in Biblical Counseling from the College of Biblical

Studies and a Certification in Christian Counseling. She resides in Pearland, Texas.

Learn more at her website, KachelleKelly.com.

CHAPTER TEN

DREAM, PRAY, HUSTLE YOUR WAY TO AUTHORPRENEURSHIP

Kachelle Kelly

I wrote my first book, *Pretty Painful,* in 2005, a book that answers the question, "Can looks really kill who you are?" (The answer is yes.) In it, I debunk the whole myth that says seemingly beautiful or prosperous or powerful people experience no problems at all.

I felt very strongly that I had to get this message out, but I didn't know anything about publishing—at all! You hear the stories that you need a publisher, you need to get somebody to get behind you, but I felt like my message was so important that I did not want to wait on those opportunities to present themselves.

I scraped up all the money that I could; I even borrowed money from my parents to get a book cover done. As I wrote the book, I came up with chapters of what I wanted to cover first, and then began to write them. I wrote and put the book out in six months because I was very determined to get it done. It was just something that was burning in my heart.

That was back in 2005 when we did not have social media as we know it today. I didn't have a way to share my book with the world. I did have a website, but only one where I paid the minimal cost to get it designed. I sold the books out the trunk of my car, and I had book signings anywhere anybody would invite me.

Then one time a school district in Beaumont invited me out, and they bought books for every student in their senior class. Actually, they read the book as a class assignment, were required to write a book report, and then I came in and spoke to them. It was a very powerful experience. As a memento, I captured that day on video.

Pretty Painful actually did very well without social media —it was just little old me sending emails to my email list, doing book signings everywhere, speaking, and doing radio. I was telling everyone that I had this message, and I wanted to get it out to the people. I think that's a lot of what goes wrong when people write a book; they write a book, and then they go, "Now what?" Or they write a book and say, "Who's going to read this?" When you have a message so important, you must be deliberate in promoting the fact that everybody needs to read your book—even if this requires you to kick the door down to make sure that people are reading it. Do what you must to get into the hands of the people who need it! It will change their lives.

I think that when you talk about the top ten suggestions for authorpreneurs, that's one of mine.

That's how I started my journey as an authorpreneur, and it brought in a lot of income for me. Then in 2012, a publishing company saw that *Pretty Painful* was doing very well and offered me a publishing deal.

With my current book, *Boss Women and Men Pray*, it was one of those things where it came to me like a download from God. I started doing research to see if there was anything like it on the market, and saw that there wasn't anything on how to marry success with the works of the Holy Spirit. We readily talk about our businesses, but we never talk about what keeps us spiritually grounded, what keeps us encouraged, because we don't have a lot of business owners around who feel comfortable doing so.

This book project was something that was very near and dear to my heart. I wanted this book to be one of those staple books like *Think & Grow Rich* or *Who Moved My Cheese?*— you know, books that are timeless.

I am happy to say that today people associate *Boss Women and Men Pray* with those other books that are must-haves in your success library.

I have found that if you want to be successful in your business, in life, then you must incorporate prayer in your hustle. That is the direction you have to go. This wasn't exactly what I set out to do, but it kind of organically happened, and I caught up with God's vision: *Boss Women & Men Pray* is now doing phenomenally well.

There's one thing that people really don't understand: You've got to get a cover done, you've got to get the inside laid out, you've got to get it on Kindle, you've got to get an ISBN. All of these things that people really don't know about *cost money*, but you have to do them to make the book marketable.

I did the cover for *Boss Women & Men Pray* first, and advertised it. I didn't have the money to design the interior of the book, but I presold copies of it. I then teased my readership with tidbits that were in the book to get people interested in the content. I presold enough copies to pay for all of my fees to actually print the book.

If you are an entrepreneur with a great product or service you want to sell and you want it to be successful, you have to believe that you have something that the world needs. You must be willing to do anything to make that happen and put it in the hands of people who really need it. You must exert the same type of energy when you write a book.

Aspiring authors think that their book is supposed to be something they just write, and then they can kind of sit back and exhale because they've completed some great accomplishment. But it is not an accomplishment if it is not in the readers' hands … and you have to work hard to make it happen. You have to be an *authorpreneur*. It's not about you writing the book; it's not about you saying, "Oh, I wrote a book!" You are now becoming an *author*, so you *call* yourself an author. When people ask you what you do, you don't say, "I wrote a book," you say, "I am an author." You have to push the book, and you have to get help in whatever area you need to do that.

Fast forward to today, where we now have multiple social media outlets. I have sold so many copies of my books on the social media platform! When I was seeking out help in publishing, a publishing company here in Houston told me that the average self-published book sells a thousand copies a year. I am currently, all praises to God, selling that in a month to month-and-a-half, give or take, for *Boss Women & Men Pray*!

I started preselling this book in December 2013, and it sold consistently in 2014. Doing the same thing in 2015, I expect it to go to even greater heights. I have now acquired a publishing contract, and I am going to come out with a workbook, an audio book, and a second edition with four new chapters to expand on the things that I do in hindsight that people can really benefit from.

The extra material deals strictly with my personal trials as an entrepreneur; for example, when I went through such a dramatic time with my dad dying—literally dying—*twice* on Thanksgiving. People followed the story of my faith and my determination to see my father live. I literally had to put my business on hold, attempting to not lose money but make money with the book in the midst of everything. This is a sample of the testimonies that I need-ed to add into the book of how storms are going to come in your life, even when you are an author and entrepreneur. But I also want people to see that in spite of those storms, you have to stay the course and believe that things are going to work out for you and your project.

As for promotion, I recently came up with an idea of doing a photo shoot that included thirty of Houston's top rappers, party promoters, real estate agents, pastors, and politicians. I did a photo shoot with Boss Women and Men from all across the city. The promotional T-shirts I created were a way to get my brand across and to make money. I now have a T-shirt and candles to sell. I also have the workbook and the audio book coming, speaking engagements, and seminars to teach people how Boss Women and Men really do pray. All of these are extensions of my business—writing in business journals, writing blogs, all of this I do so that it points readers back to my book. I even have audios that I do for each chapter in the book, and I did what I call a month-long book club for people to buy the book to enjoy with their friends and to get their friends together in this movement. That's the component that I added to bring in more sales, and to give people a direct connection to me. I wanted them to know the heart and soul behind what it is that I've written.

The book club was very successful, so much so that I had to create a website along with a book called BossesPray. com. This is the website that people can go to at any time whether they have read the book or not, where they get daily audios of me talking about the book and encouraging them, giving them even more information that I did not put in the book. It also gives them videos as well, that they can also find on my YouTube channel.

That's another thing: launch a YouTube channel where you can dive into places that you can't dive into on paper—video connects people with people. I have gained clients just through my book because I tell them to schedule a thirty-minute free session with me on my website.

I have created the Boss Men and Women Pray movement, and part of being a living testimony of that movement is to demonstrate the power of what I wrote about: prayer. No matter what background or field you come from, you can pray and you can profess that God is the CEO of your business.

It's humbling to know that I've started a movement that has and will continue to revolutionize the lives of small business owners across the world. I gave my all to this book project, which often took me into uncharted territory, and I have prospered as a result. My prayer for you is that you will become as tenacious about the pursuit of your success as I was and reap a similar harvest of success.

Remember, REAL Boss Women and Men pray!

Carla R. Cannon, also known as "The Trailblazer" and Transformational Coach, is dedicated to empowering, equipping, and strengthening women on how to operate in their divine calling authentically and in a spirit of excellence from the pulpit to the marketplace. She is also a national bestselling author and high level book coach. Through her company Inspiring Hearts Coaching Institute, she develops aspiring authors into published authors by teaching them how to write, publish, and market their book by sharing their story from a place of power rather than pain or pity.

Carla is a woman who is all about connectivity and building a community where Christ is at the center and women of every culture can come together in unity to build, expand, and further one another.

Contact her at CarlaCannon.com and on all major social media outlets @CarlaRCannon.

CHAPTER ELEVEN
YOUR PAIN HAS PURPOSE

Carla R. Cannon

My journey as an authorpreneur began without me actually having any acknowledgement of it. I never desired to write to gain a profit but only to transform the lives of others and empower them with my story.

Years before I began writing my first book, *The Power in Waiting*, my life was one of great intensity and confusion. I found myself in an identity crisis, great depression, and in a state of suicide where I was simply tired of living. I remember begging God to take my life because I knew I didn't want to commit suicide, for, according to the Holy Bible, that one act alone would send me on a direct trip to Hell, in which I would spend eternity. Growing up in church, I knew this was not the path I truly desired to take, but I couldn't seem to free myself from the pain I was experiencing now on a daily basis.

I remember writing down my thoughts, which I now look back and identify as desperate cries and prayers unto the Lord. I was a broken and deeply wounded individual. Growing up with my father in and out of my life due to his struggle with alcohol abuse caused me to lack the validation of my father, which every girl should receive rather than having to grow up seeking it from one individual to the next. In addition I was also labeled as ADHD and being Behaviorally Emotionally Handicapped; I was placed in special classes with children whose IQs were extremely low and who wore helmets and had cloths attached to them to capture their slobber that often dripped from their mouths. I was placed in this class not because I wasn't smart—the various tests I often underwent with my therapist proved that I was a very intelligent young girl—it was my behavior.

My placement there played heavily upon my psyche. I remember growing up feeling as if I was crazy. I can recall teachers telling me I would never amount to anything because I was so bad in school, according to them. But what I was really was a young, battered girl who was being physically abused by her step-father, and who watched her mother be abused as well. Not once do I remember one teacher sitting me down and asking what was going on at home. There had to be a reason why I was so rebellious and defiant … but no one had enough discernment to ask. They only assumed I knew better but never really found a way to get to the core of the issue except for placing me on Ritalin, a medication that suppressed my appetite and made me feel weird. My teachers loved it because it kept me out of their hair and I was quiet, although I was ultimately suffering in silence because the medication basically controlled me. I barely said two words or moved out of my seat while under this "hypnosis."

In the midst of the abuse, God would always send a certain teacher who would love on me and speak life to me, but they were far and in between. I'll never forget an old principal who used to treat me as if I were her own daughter. I also had another teacher I used to stay with who was a Caucasian woman. She was really nice to me and had a beautiful home. I remember staying with her during some school nights, and she would always have soft, warm Jimmy Dean biscuits waiting for me at the table. I often think of her; last I heard she had cancer, but I've always prayed that the Lord would allow our paths to cross so I could simply tell her thank you.

Fast forward a bit. I later ended up pregnant and gave birth to my daughter at eighteen. I was simply a baby having a baby. To cause even greater devastation, three months after my daughter was born, her father (the man I thought would be my husband) and I broke up. It left me broken, feeling abandoned and back to a familiar place of rejection. During this time I became promiscuous, was driven by my pain, and completely lost my identity.

Due to never actually dealing with my issues, I found myself in same-sex relationships, which took place for a period of five years of my life. During that time alcohol and marijuana became my coping mechanism. Thankfully, that portion of my life didn't last long because I did not like being addicted to anything; it reminded me of my childhood medication that was supposed to "help" me but only crippled me and added to my issues. I also saw how drugs and alcohol negatively affected my father's life, and I wanted no parts of it.

All the pain, abuse, abandonment, rejection, and various mistakes I made is where *Women of Standard Magazine* was birthed.[1] God taught me how to transform my pain into power by teaching me how to submit to my process, confront my issues, and make the necessary decisions needed in order to conquer what stared me back in the face on a daily basis. I'd have to say my road to authorpreneurship began by my being led by the Holy Spirit to share my story, which in return and to my surprise helped set thousands of women free!

I always say God set me up, because He allowed me to go through these things since He knew I could handle it and knew I wouldn't be afraid to share my experiences and expose my weaknesses and vulnerabilities in an effort to help others become free of the very things that once held me captive.

I later became an ordained minister and underwent an ordination service, officially becoming a minister of the Gospel of Jesus Christ, and I began to share the amazing transformation the Lord had done in my life. It kind of reminded me of Saul's experience on the Damascus road with his encounter with God. It was in that moment that Saul officially came to the end of himself, which brought him to a place in which he totally surrendered unto the Lord. It was as if I had finally come to the end of myself and finally said "Yes, Lord" from the very depths of my spirit.

In March 2013, I published my first book, *The Power in Waiting*, which I wrote in a process of seven days. I will never forget those days, for they were days of many tears, remembering many hurts, but also where my ultimate healing began to take place. That one book transformed my entire life; in sharing my story, my book became not only an Amazon bestselling book but also made the National Bestsellers List for Black Christian Authors. It completely blew my mind! I never knew that by sharing my story, I would set so many women free … and that so many would be able to relate and desire to connect with me because of it. In that moment I realized I needed to continue to share where I had been, what I had done, and how God had literally used my pain and transformed it into power!

A year later I released my second book, *A Single Woman's Focus: Every Ruth Needs a Naomi*, which also went on to become an Amazon bestselling book, touching the lives of many single women across the globe. Here I shared my struggles specifically as a single woman, and it was amazing how many women could relate to my stories and struggle of living the single life as not only a Christian but also a minister.

By this time my platform was developed, my voice was being heard, and my brand was being noticed. But guess what? It all began with my passion and desire to serve others.

Today, I am on book number three, *Write the Book Already! How to Write a Best Selling Book in 7 Days*, in which I help aspiring authors to become published authors by encouraging them to share their story from a place of power rather than pain. Through this book I am teaching others how to identify with their story, share it strategically, write their book in seven days, develop their own platform as a speaker, and much more!

Today I also run and operate my own company, Carla R. Cannon Enterprises, which houses my publishing company, Cannon Publishing, as well as my book coaching firm, Inspiring Hearts Coaching Institute.[2] All of this is to say that because I shared my story unapologetically, I have had the opportunity to share my story before hundreds of women; in fact, I believe there will come a day very soon in which I will minister and speak before thousands of people.

But how did I do this? What's more, how can you have similar success?

For me, I had to first own my experiences by facing them head on; as Paula White says, it is impossible to conquer what one is unwilling to confront. I also had to understand that I am my sister, meaning everything I have ever experienced was never about me but to help motivate, empower, strengthen, and encourage others, particularly women.

My journey as an authorpreneur has been one of great courage and faith, for I believe that anything is possible and that we were born with everything we need placed inside of us. If we would learn to simply tap into it and stop seeking external things to define and compliment us, we can operate in our divine calling a lot sooner and without all the extra baggage that we ultimately bring upon ourselves.

The purpose of me sharing my story with you is to show that everything you have experienced in life that has caused you much pain, embarrassment, or the tears to roll down your face were all for the purpose of you strengthening, encouraging, or helping someone else to overcome their darkest hours. There is indeed purpose in your pain; my assignment and central focus is to ignite the fire within you, which in turn will give you the courage to step out on faith and share your story to help save someone else or who may currently reside where you have once been as well.

Know that it will not be easy and that you may feel afraid. But true courage is stepping out in spite of the presence of fear. National televangelist Joyce Meyer encourages us to "do it afraid." What that means is never wait on fear to go away, but even in its presence, you square your should-ers back, crack your knuckles, and get ready to give the enemy (your adversary) the greatest blow by taking all of your pain and strategically developing your story in an effort to help others.

Remember, friends: your pain has power. Now go and share it, and when you do, I will be here to welcome you to the world of being an authorpreneur!

Roxana Heredia has been a language professional for ten years, having worked as a Spanish bilingual teacher for several years and as a translator. A native Spanish speaker, Roxana earned a BA in Spanish from the University of Houston, and obtained her Master's Degree in Public Relations from George Washington University.

After working for many years as a Spanish bilingual teacher, Roxana used her teaching and language skills to found LISTO Translating Services & More, LLC. In her role at LISTO, Roxana manages a large network of translators, interpreters, editors, and proofreaders, as well as the overall translation workflow methodology and interpretation assignment planning. She ensures that the right people, processes, and resources are applied to each project. Her goal is to help people to break down any language barriers they may come across in order to enhance their personal and professional lives.

Roxana was recently appointed by Houston's mayor, Annise Parker, to serve on the mayor's Hispanic Advisory Board because of her service to both the English-speaking and Hispanic communities.

CHAPTER TWELVE
BRIDGING THE LANGUAGE DIVIDE

Roxana Heredia

I started working as a bilingual teacher in the public school system. Parents would come to me because they wanted to me translate school documents to be able to help their children and be an interpreter at special education ARD meetings. Because of the language barrier and because they saw the teacher as an authority, as someone who can be relied on not just to help their children but to help them, they would come to me for advice. Then, of course, they wanted me to write letters and translate general documents from Spanish into English. That was my first exposure to professionally translating for others.

I came to this country at the tender age of eighteen from Lima, Peru, with my family. We experienced firsthand the language problems immigrants experience when they arrive in a new country. As a result I made it my mission to eradicate that problem. After arriving in the United States,

I earned a Bachelor of Arts Degree in Spanish from the University of Houston, and obtained my Master's Degree in Public Relations from George Washington University. I used my teaching and language skills to form LISTO Translating Services & More, LLC, in 2012.

Mastering the language divide was very critical to my family, but it is also paramount for authorpreneurs who want to expand their reach to the global market. In the literary world, breaking the language and cultural barrier is crucial, since it is imperative to build trust with your readers of all languages.

HOUSTON—A FUTURISTIC VIEW OF AMERICA

Houston is one of the most diverse cities in the country. In fact, according to the Kinder Institute from Rice University, on their last survey, Houston is what America's going to look like in the year 2050. It's imperative, then, that you translate your book manuscript into the native language of your desired audience, and also any marketing information materials, to accommodate the changing consumer demographic….

The Hispanic community is going to continue growing more and more and more—which means we're going to be one of the largest consumer groups in America.

Don't feel intimidated when attempting to get to know other cultures in other communities. While you are connecting with other cultures, you are going to be able to learn more about them.

Sometimes we feel intimidated because of the language barrier; we don't know what the people are actually saying or may be feeling. If you get to know that person, by learning their language or trying to communicate with them, you are going to feel like they are just like any other new friend you meet.

LANGUAGE BARRIER PROHIBITORS

So, one of the challenges that professional authorpreneurs may have, due to technology, is getting an accurate translation of their material. Thanks to technology, there are writers that will assist you in translating, and you must be able to ensure that other people will understand what you're trying to say.

If a translation is done by software or a machine, though, it may be missing the human element. What those machines do is just translate the document literally, word by word. They don't have the same ability a human being does to be able to convey and send the real message. What often happens is that some authors don't understand that. They say, "Well, it will be cheaper to just use Google translate or any of those translation software programs," vs. using my or someone else's services—a person, a human being, to do the translation. (And they have to be a *professional* translator—author's often don't understand that it's critical to speak someone's native tongue vs. just getting a literal translation.)

Another misconception is when people say, "I am bilingual." Often they don't understand the difference between being bilingual and being biliterate.

A bilingual person is someone that can communicate or understand the language, and interpret it. A biliterate is a person who can speak, write, and read the language—actually both languages. Because of this, what often happens is I see translations where there are several misspellings. In Spanish, for instance, if you put the accent mark on a different syllable, the meaning of the word will change, but if you aren't *biliterate* in Spanish, you wouldn't see the difference, and think that's the right way to spell the word. But your meaning is now completely different ... which could be a very bad thing!

I believe that every time you want to do a project, you need to ask questions of people that are experts in that field. It's like when you're sick: if you have heart problems, you're going to go to a cardiologist, not a dentist. If you have teeth problems, you do go to a dentist because they are the experts. The same thing applies if you're going to write a book. You need to go to people that are experts if you want to promote your book correctly. I also believe a lot in networking; go to the people that are experts in helping authors because that's how you learn and that's how you're going to have more success.

MY RECENT JOURNEY AS AN AUTHORPRENEUR

When I was invited to participate and collaborate on a compilation book, *Share Your Message with the World*, it was actually my first experience as an author. Like I mentioned before, I used to help people by translating their documents into English, so it was a nice experience because I could talk about my own challenges of facing the language barrier in this country. I also got to discuss how I overcame those challenges to be the successful authorpreneur that I am now. I had the opportunity to meet other authors, and they also wanted to spread their message across other languages. They thought of a new idea or a point-of-view, and wanted other people to read about it and learn about their ideas and their thoughts.

We live in a global economy, so people are very diverse and come from different cultures who speak different languages. Therefore, the more languages you translate your book into, the more people that are going to be able to know you, able to learn about your ideas, or whatever your message is that you want to spread.

The first time I actually wrote and published a book, I didn't know what the process was. After *Share Your Message with the World* was published, all the coauthors worked together trying to promote the book, but after the initial launch, it was up to you to promote your chapter or your book.

I implemented several strategies to let people know about what I was doing, and why I did it. Trying to explain or let people know what your idea or message is critical to getting your message out to the masses. For me it was breaking down the language barrier, which I always talk about because that's why I opened my language company. So I started writing press releases—I have made professional alliances that are very good in helping me with press releases. Then I went to different media outlets and let them know about my book.

The first time I sent out releases, one of them was picked up by the *Houston Chronicle*, and they wrote an article about my book. I started talking more about myself and how I became an entrepreneur, and I wrote more press releases. Since then I've been invited as a guest on Fox 26 News with Houston Community College, a new channel, and also with Univision, an internationally recognized Spanish broadcasting company.

The most important message that I want to leave with you is that if you have enough tenacity, you can overcome any obstacles that you're going to encounter in your life.

It is up to you to do it; be persistent and don't let anything stop you.

Shelley R. Roth is the president of Springboard Social Media, an entrepreneur and social media trainer, speaker, consultant, and author who is dedicated to helping individuals, organizations, and teams improve marketing effectiveness and sales results via social media. Springboard's methodologies and services are based on over twenty-five years of successful business development, sales, and educational leadership of individuals, early stage companies, small businesses, and Fortune 500 corporations.

Shelley's ability to inspire and empower students, partners, affiliates, and clients is recognized by all those that she works with. Shelley has a BS in Education and holds MEds in Educational Psychology and Educational Administration.

Her books are available on Amazon and her website at ShelleyRoth.com.

CHAPTER THIRTEEN

SOCIAL MEDIA: THE HEARTBEAT OF AN AUTHORPRENEUR

Shelley R. Roth

I have authored two books, over three hundred fifty video blogs, and dozens of articles as requested over the last eight years of Springboard Social Media. My latest venture, which Sharon Jenkins has gladly and willingly participated in, is Funday School for Business via Google+ Hangouts. At Funday School we shared a lively discussion via video panel on the conscious business practice introduced at the start of each hangout, public, live, and on air. Our topics included: Give to Grow; Scarcity to Abundance; Defining What Value is in Business and How We Recognize it; and seven more topics over the 2014 year. (These hangouts are being combined into a best practices for business book coming out in the summer of 2015. Sharon, of course, will be part of that book.)

I started my social media business in the spring of 2006. What drove me was wanting to get back to my roots as a teacher and combine this with my passion for business (small business in particular). When I started, very few businesses had incorporated social media into their marketing mix, so I created course curriculum to teach business owners how to use social media to bring their business to the social networking markets.

The first class was a sellout, and I knew I was onto something. The next step, after creating and delivering curriculum for all the top social networks such as LinkedIn, Facebook, and Twitter, was to author a book. I realized that it was all about being authentic when participating in social networks, and thus my first book, *Get Real, People! How to Use Social Media for REAL-ationship Marketing*. I had never authored a book before; however, I knew people were clamoring and thirsting for knowledge on social media, so thus began my journey as an authorpreneur, and off I went!

Get Real, People! is about why being your authentic, "real" self online (and, of course, in person) trumps anything you could ever create and pretend to be. Social media, in 2011, was creating a change in how marketing was being accomplished. It brought on the advent that social media relationships were an asset that was difficult to measure the ROI—Return on Investment—of, but definitely contributed to the Return on Influence. Businesses were starting to realize this digital world was hard to read like the world of physical body language. How do you ensure and communicate your real self online? And how do you know if others are being real? Sometimes there are "wolves in sheep's clothing" out there. I met one of them online and that is what put me on the path of writing the book in the first place.

The book also includes tips on how to use social media to build community and businesses with longer lasting, more meaningful engagement and relationships. It also addresses findings on how to read people's "digital body language" and what certain behaviors say about you and your business.

The most fun for me was the marketing of the book. We had six events in a twenty-four-hour period: we were live via Facebook chat for six hours; I was on three radio shows that day; I did a live book signing that evening; and we were posting like crazy on all the top social networks to get the word out about the book. It was a lot of fun, and *Get Real, People!* made it to No. 6 on Amazon during that twenty-four-hour period.

Writing the book was also very enjoyable. I love to teach people how to use social media, and interviewing dozens of people about digital body language was a blast. I felt like a reporter!

Publishing, on the other hand, was challenging. I self-published using Amazon's CreateSpace, and had both a hard copy and digital version of the book. I was fortunate to have an editor that helped every step of the way in editing and also submitting documents to CreateSpace. The revisions were many; however, as Sharon would say, there is nothing like "birthing a book"!

This experience brought me to my second book, published in 2012, *Shedding Your Sales Shark: Lessons from a Recovering Sales Shark & How to Apply Them to Social Media Marketing & Life*. That is a mouthful for a title, but it states clearly what the book is about. I was in sales most of my adult life, and I was a darn good salesperson. However, in my heart, I really didn't care about the close; I cared about the relationship. I was a farmer not a hunter ... And, like with social media, it's all about building those relationships.

This second book talks about how social media has completely shifted the sales and marketing landscape and how business gets done. Corporate environments often thrive on an intense "eat what you kill" approach. The inclusive community-driven nature of social media is sending traditional sales sharks, and their shark tanks, the way of the dinosaur. *Shedding Your Sales Shark*, though, was designed for those looking for effective ways to engage with their clients and community via social media networks. As a recovering sales shark, I shared my discovery of how social media's demand to be transparent opens doors to creating new abundance in business and in life. This book shares differences between the qualities and behaviors of a sales shark vs. a relationship builder; also included are real-life stories of sales sharks who left the shark tank to follow their dreams and live their passion and purpose.

I self-published *Shedding Your Sales Shark* using CreateSpace as well. I must admit, the second birth was easier than the first! Now, in 2014, I have continued to help hundreds of business people and nonprofits grow their businesses using social media marketing. Course work and strategy work on Facebook, LinkedIn, Pinterest, Video Content Marketing, Twitter, and more have been instrumental in helping people and businesses' growth.

My next goal is to take the last eleven months of 2014's Funday School and "birth" book three (as yet untitled). While that happens, I leave you with these last thoughts for your authorpreneurship journey:

1. Be accountable to your word

2. Be consistent

3. Be unstoppable

4. Let no one tell you no

5. Listen to your heart

6. Get help, as it takes a village

7. Define your market

8. Market via social media and other channels

9. Don't write a book to make money

10. Read 1-9

Melanie Bragg is the author of *Crosstown Park*, a social legal thriller with a spiritual twist. She has long enjoyed a reputation as one of Houston's fiercest attorneys in her representation of children, the elderly, and mentally disadvantaged people. Her firm, Bragg Law PC, is a general civil firm in Houston, Texas. She also writes and produces legal education programs through Legal Insight, Inc. Her writing credits include *HIPAA for the General Practitioner*, published by the American Bar Association, as well as the upcoming book *Defining Moments: Insights into the Lawyers Soul*, to be published by the American Bar Association Flagship Division. She was the Author 101 University Success Story featured speaker in 2012 and is a frequent speaker and teacher to groups of lawyers, writers, and business professionals.

When she's not writing, Melanie devotes her time to her work as Chair of the Book Publications Board of the Solo, Small Firm & General Practice Division, and sharing ideas with fellow authors.

She is a Professional Member of the National Speakers Association and serves on the NSA-Houston Board of Directors as Secretary. On Friday afternoons you can see her at the local movie theater catching a new movie. If you look real hard, you will see a big smile on her face.

She can be reached at Melanie@melaniebragg.com or her website, MelanieBragg.com.

CHAPTER FOURTEEN
MAXIMIZE YOUR AUTHOR EXPERIENCE

Melanie Bragg

The road to becoming an author can start early—like it did for me in second grade when I typed the *Story of my Life* in red ink on my mother's typewriter—or it can start much later. But one thing is for certain—being an author in today's times is much more than typing away at your desk and then sending the manuscript by snail-mail to a publisher with an in-house editor who will correct all of your typos, then print and market it for you. For an author to sit back and receive big fat royalty checks is a thing of the past; I am not sure it ever existed.

The bottom line is: *Being an author is a lot of work.* You have to really love it and do everything you need to do in order to be successful. And, in fact, the writing part of being an author is just the beginning.

The word "authorpreneur" encompasses the skills required to be an author in today's world. Writers come in all shapes and sizes. They find time to write on the bus, the train, before work, in between shifts—whatever it takes to get the job done. It is the *love* of writing that keeps them going.

In recent years the publishing world has undergone a radical transformation. The industry is still in transition. Agents and traditional publishers are changing the way they do things. Anyone with the tenacity to actually sit down and write their manuscript, *and* with ample funds in their pocketbook, can get published. The big publishing houses are keeping up with the times by opening their own self-publishing branches.

Authors, too, have different motivations for getting published. Some just want to tell their stories or get their message across: Vanity Press. Or they want to tell someone else's story: True Crime/Biography. Others want to be the female John Grisham: Melanie Bragg. Some think they have written or will write the "great American novel." The truth is that most everyone has a book in them, and if you are a writer, you have probably been approached by folks with a "great idea" for a book they want *you* to write for them. I tell them to learn the *craft* of writing and dig in. Most writers I know already have their stories in mind and are busy working to accomplish their own goals.

There is a wealth of information on the market today about the *craft* of writing. In his book *On Writing*, Steven King gives a great overview of the process. I was lucky to have the late, great Rita Gallagher, cofounder of RWA (Romance

Writers of America) teach me the craft of fiction writing and novel structure. The education was priceless. I remember fondly the four years of spending all day every Friday soaking up her wisdom. She will always be my writing angel, and the picture of her inward and outward beauty is in my mind's eye when I write. I can hear her say, "Every word is a dollar to an editor" to teach me that less is best.

Here is the good news: Sugar coating the hard work involved doesn't help anyone. But there is no doubt that accomplishing your life-long dream of publishing a book and being satisfied with the quality of the book is, what I call, the "elixir of accomplishing your true purpose in life."

For me, someone who was born to write, all of the effort is worth it, and I would not trade it for anything in the world. I want to share my lessons learned so that you will be better prepared to have success in your writing career.

So here we go for the "best practices" I want you to know *now*.

WRITERS MUST LEARN TO LISTEN TO OTHERS ...

… but to always follow their own gut.

People are well-meaning most of the time, but sometimes they just plain don't know what they are talking about. It is kind of like asking your spouse to edit your book—boy, is that ever a setup; of course they are going to love it! An impartial, disinterested person should always be your editor.

But what I mean here is that you should always know that your judgment as an author is best. It is good to get information from books, teachers, and critique groups, but in the final analysis, if you feel strongly about something in your manuscript, you should go with it.

I learned this from my critique group. Everything I debated with my teacher to keep in would be the very thing every month that the class loved. It taught me to take the teacher's advice or the students' feedback, but to keep the things I felt very strongly about because they would resonate with audiences.

An example of this was the beginning of my first novel, *Crosstown Park.* Everything you read about starting a novel says that you have to start with a big impact, a big crisis, so my first draft started with a courtroom scene. It never resonated with me, and I felt very strongly that the story starts when Alex meets the reverend on a plane. It was the most important part of the story, even though it was not a big climax or catastrophe, because it was the beginning of a major shift in the main character's life. Sometimes those events can be subtle and seem small, but in retrospect they are life-changing. In the final version, I went with my gut to stay with the plane scene and was so pleased when so many readers commented that they loved how the story began. Two points for me following my own best judgment. Do the same in your work, and you will be happy and turn out a better final product.

WRITERS MUST DEVELOP A ...

... marketing plan with their vision, a framework, and a build-out plan.

I teach a class on this, but let me say that you have to start with your *vision*.

- How do you see yourself and the book once it is done?
- What are your goals for the book?
- Do you want to keep writing after this project?
- Do you know the reality of how much it costs?
- How much time it takes?
- How long it takes to get the pay off? What is the pay off?
- Have you really researched the business?
- Are you realistic about your vision and your goals?

Taking a deep breath and giving it some deep thought here will go a long way.

Many people think writing is easy until they try. They think that making an A on a paper in high school English makes them a writer. I actually thought that. Rita used to look up at me when I was impatient during class and say, "How long did it take you to be a lawyer?" I would say, "Four years of college and three years of law school." She would say, "Did you really think you could be a writer with no effort?" I would always shrug my shoulders and give her a sheepish grin and say, "Yes." After a while I got the message that the "sweat equity" in writing is the same as anything else in life. You have to be your own Rocky Balboa and "Just do it!"

The *framework* is what you do to learn the craft, what writing groups you join, what events you attend, and what you learn about the business of writing. Planning in advance, knowing who your market is, and making sure you have nonfiction hooks in your fiction so you have lots of things to talk to audiences about is crucial in this phase.

The *build-out* is the fun part after publication. If you have done the vision and the framework well, then you will have fun. During the build-out you are speaking and doing events all the time and really getting the word out on your book. You cannot wait and plan everything after the book comes out. It is an organic process, and as much as you plan, other things happen. It is truly a delightful experience and one you want to enjoy. I did twenty-one events in ninety days after my novel came out, and I learned an incredible amount about being an author in a very short period of time. I had to muster all of the strength and confidence I had and then enjoyed the ride.

After all, I spent many years creatively visualizing the day when I would be the author in a Barnes & Noble store. I can honestly say the reality is every bit as good as the dream, and when I am doing a book event, I feel as authentic as I can be. I am the person I was born to be.

With *Crosstown Park*, I spent the time establishing relationships with the store CRMs—the community relations managers—so that when the sequel, *All One Blood*, comes out, I will be welcomed back with open arms.

One word about bookstores: I focused on selling my books, but more than that, I focused on giving the customers in the store a good experience with me, the author. That is what the stores like. They want to be seen in the community as supporting authors and providing interesting authors to their customers.

Remember, it is a marathon, not a jog.

One CRM told me a story about how Deepak Chopra stayed at a book signing until 1:00 a.m., until the last person was taken care of. When the CRM thanked him, Deepak said, "It is my honor. I still remember the days when I came in and sat at a table and no one even stopped to talk to me."

I loved that the CRM shared that story with me because it made me feel like he understood that all authors start somewhere. If Deepak Chopra went through what I am going through, then it is all right. You just have to keep going—get up on the horse and stay in the saddle.

WRITERS MUST BECOME INTERESTED IN ...

... and support other writers. Become an activist—get involved in books! Join your local writing groups, get in a critique group, read magazines, sign up for blogs, look outside your genre. It is important to learn the craft and to know what is going on out there. Build your platform and your following. Make sure the people you meet are added to your list. Ask them, "May I put you on a list to receive notices of my book signings?" Write a blog. Send out newsletters.

And promote other authors. When people see you promoting other authors, you become the go-to guy or girl in the business. People want to hear from you because you are in the know. This is your world—be a leader.

Some authors just live in a vacuum and only think of their book. But the really successful ones I know are active. They support other authors online and in social marketing groups. It is kind of a "scratch my back" and "I'll scratch yours" world, so the more you spread the word about others who may be ahead of you, the more people you will have behind you in terms of spreading the word about your endeavors. If you are an island, it will be very lonely when the book comes out and does not sell.

Surround yourself with people who want what you want and help them get where they are going; you will get farther. You don't have to get it back directly from those you give to, though, and if you think you will, you will be disappointed. Think of it as sowing lots of seeds so that there will be a harvest for you when the time comes.

WRITERS MUST DEVELOP ...

... multimedia skills and social marketing skills. You must have a strong online presence with Facebook, Linkedin, Google+, Goodreads, Amazon, Instagram, Pinterest, and any other site relevant to your market.

If you are saying to yourself that you don't like Facebook —*stop it!* Facebook is an invaluable tool. And I promise, I do not spend that much time on Facebook. I have managed to integrate it into my life as a pleasurable activity that does not take long. It is paying out big dividends.

Social marketing does not always work instantly, and you do not always get instant feedback on it, but plug ahead anyway. And like I said above, keep giving. You "like" people's stuff, you comment on their threads, and they will come to you and their friends will come to you. Take courses that make it easier for you, and learn simple things all the time.

One example I can give you is one day when I walked into court and several people asked me about *Crosstown Park*; they had all seen it on Facebook. The word had spread with little effort on my part other than to post photos of my book events. I had reached what felt like a celebrity status and didn't even know it.

People are watching whether they comment or not. They respect you for following through on your dream.

The value of social marketing is not always apparent, but don't let that stop you! Develop a practice of spending a little time in the morning and a little time in the evening on It and it will multiply.

One word of caution: Don't over-post. Let your public miss you and wonder what exciting things you have been doing while you have been offline. You can create a lot of buzz that way. The mystery of you...

WRITERS MUST BE ...

... their own publicist (or hire one at several thousand dollars a pop).

If you have a big budget, you can hire a publicist, but make sure and research them thoroughly. Make sure you know what they are going to do for you, talk to some of their other clients, and be fully aware going in what your duties are and what their duties are. I have not heard a lot of great publicist stories, and since I am such a natural self-promoter, I have not met the right person for the right price to promote me ... yet.

You are the best person to promote you. Mind your blog, promote your book, and do everything you can to have the most visibility.

WRITERS MUST BECOME ...

... public speakers.

To be a successful author, it is imperative that you can speak in front of a group and give a good talk. After *Crosstown Park* came out, doing twenty-one events in ninety days taught me real fast that you need to have a plan, and you need to follow that plan and then leave room for what happens in the group dynamic.

The place to start getting time in front of an audience is one of your many local Toastmasters groups. When you get a little more polished, I would suggest the National Speakers Association chapter in your locale. I qualified to become a Professional Speaker with the organization and got on the Board of my local chapter, NSA Houston, which put me in touch with the monthly speakers. I get invited to the speaker dinners and lunches, so my skills as a speaker are growing due to my involvement … plus I get to fellowship with like-minded folks. There are lots of coaches, and each meeting is a workshop on a different aspect of public speaking, teaching us skills all authors need to know about, like storytelling. These skills will come in handy at your author events. Plus it helps you build your "list."

There are many different forms of author events. There are pre-launch parties, launch parties, book signings, book events, book panels, book fairs, book festivals, book conferences, and book clubs to name a few. What you talk about is different for each one, and you have to use a different set of skills. For some of them, you talk to a group, some of them you talk to individuals, but no matter where, you have to learn how to talk about your book in the best way. You have to enroll people into wanting to read the book.

It can be a challenge to talk about yourself and your book all the time, even for the outgoing types like myself. But at the events you have to be able to talk to and respond to a variety of people, all the while fielding questions about the book.

The most frequently asked question is, "How long did it take to write?" You want to create a compelling story around this inevitable question. There are many paths to choose here, and I confess I did mine by trial and error until I came up with what feels comfortable to me. Don't think you have to come up with something new each time. Think about how little kids like to hear the same story over and over. Audiences are the same. Hone your stories and tell them time and time again.

The audience will think of things you never thought of when you wrote the book. And you have to be prepared to respond to mistakes. For instance, an old high school friend of mine showed up at a book signing, and I was so excited. Then he told me, "You called the thing in the middle of the road a medium instead of a median." He thought it was a typographical error; in fact, it was intentional, and my editor did not catch it. (Note to self: editors are humans too.) I always thought the middle of the road was a medium! What an enlightened moment I had when I learned otherwise for the first time. Instead of being upset about the mistake, though, I enjoyed it and the crowd appreciated that I did not defend it or try to explain it away. Audiences love us when we are human. The more vulnerable you are, the more fun you will have.

The audience also wants to know how you came up with the idea for the story and a little bit about the background of the story. I have tried out many different aspects of the process with a variety of groups and it depends upon your audience. That is where practice comes in handy, especially when you can rehearse in front of a supportive and impartial group before you get to the real audiences.

Next time I will be more prepared because I learned much of this when *Crosstown Park* was released a month early—and yes, I went into a panic mode when it was released a month early, though I was happy to be as prepared as I was. My goal is for you to be prepared. I want you to be the best you can be.

WRITERS MUST TAKE A DEEP BREATH ...

… place hand over heart, and repeat.

Yes—because after book one is book two. The whole process begins again. And eventually, like saving money in the bank, the work you have done begins to multiply for you. You become an established author with an audience who loves to read your books.

Does it sound tough or overwhelming? I hope you are motivated and encouraged that despite how much work it is, being a successful published author is the elixir of life, a secret potion to your enhance your long-term happiness and fulfillment.

Armchair writers or Monday morning quarterbacks will not advance your career. In fact, they can kill your dream real fast. Power through it, make a plan, stick to your plan, and follow my motto: *Never, ever give up!* You will do just fine.

CHAPTER FIFTEEN
THE PORTRAIT OF A REAL AUTHORPRENEUR

Sharon C. Jenkins

The beauty of an authorpreneur's soul is not in how much money they make or the number of books they sell but in the lives that are changed as a result of their servitude to their readers.

I compiled this collection of inspiring stories of other authorpreneurs because I wanted you to have a true representation of what constitutes a REAL authorpreneur, someone who is Relevant, Entrepreneurial, Action-Oriented, and Literary-Focused. In these pages we have painted realistic portraits of authorpreneurs who have weathered the storm of a business start-up and courted the hearts of authors for their goodwill. I salute them for having the courage to weather the journey and excel against great odds.

You have read their stories.

This is mine.

MY STORY

I have been passionate about reading since kindergarten. I loved the escape; reading allowed me to venture into places that I could only dream of going. I soon became infatuated with those who had the power to transport me to other worlds: authors. So, imagine my surprise when I discovered my own gift for writing. Not only could someone else take me to a distant land on the pages of a book, but I realized I could also do the same for others.

My mother was my earliest fan and source of support. She knew I had stumbled upon my purpose, my calling. She was glad we finally found an explanation for my vivid imagination and seemed to be the only member of our family who had a healthy appreciation for my new found talent.

My love for authors blossomed as I grew older because I was able to find voices I could relate to during my rebellious teen years—ones that supported my anti-everything position. Maya Angelou, Nikki Giovanni, and the Last Poets both intrigued and mesmerized me by their revolutionary rhymes. They inspired me to pick up a pen and write passionate discourses about pages in history that were not shared readily with strangers, and love that I could only fantasize about.

However, when real love finally captured my heart, I became enthralled with living the life of a wife and mother, suppressing my ardor for writing for a season.

As an adult I found my voice again after several life changing occurrences, the most profound among them being that I found God. Unfortunately, I lost the love of my life in the midst of it all (but that's another book...). I found therapy through poetic release, and as a result, ventured out of my writing closet to do some spoken word. I found out that I love center stage, and—equally important—I discovered that audiences love me. That prompted me to transition from poetry to playwriting, and I wrote my first Christian play, *The Café of Hope*, and then another, *Benjamin Thomas Worthington, Resurrected*. Both were well received, which gave me the courage to write a book.

My first project was a poetry book called *Songs of Three Sisters*, which I coauthored with two other sisters in Christ. My second project was a compilation called *Ready, Set, Succeed—Making Your Dream Come True*. In 2007, I released my first solo project, *Beyond the Closet Door: Christ's Rescue from Abuse*. Finally, in 2012, I released the initial version of *Authorpreneurship: The Business of Writing*.

Over the years I have contributed to numerous magazines and blogs, written and performed poetry for special occasions, and collaborated with authors on special projects. I have helped hundreds of authors get their message to the masses through workshops, webinars, my radio show, "The Literary Showcase," and coaching. In 2011, I became the consulting editor for one of the largest minority marketing and communications companies in Houston, where I helped produce three monthly journals and managed over eighty-five contributing writers from the faith-based, business, and health and wellness arena.

My passion for authors created within me a compelling desire to help aspiring writers become established in their craft. As a result I've been doing writers' workshops and summits for aspiring authors. I launched my series of signature events for writers with the Desire to Inspire writers' workshops in 2006. Inspired by the writers' book festivals I had been attending and watching the networking taking place when the foot traffic dwindled, I decided it might be a great idea to create an opportunity for authors to officially focus on networking, and the Authors Networking Summit was born in 2010 and put to rest in 2014.

My pursuit of authorpreneurship, coupled with my love for authors, is a by-product of twelve years in the classroom teaching business, computer, and marketing classes to middle school, high school, and college students. It was my observation that the typical writer is more comfortable behind the computer screen crafting tales and sharing valuable expertise rather than marketing and mastering the social media side of the business of writing. It is my purpose to infuse that writer with the tools to become the literary superheroes that they write about.

After I retired as an educator, I became a freelance writer and founded The Master Communicator & Associates in 2006; in 2012, that transitioned to The Master Communicator's Writing Services and a senior publishing consultant with Ellechor Media. I've studied, taught, and practiced the methodology of business for over twenty years and incorporated a "lessons learned" approach to the way I do business. I want to help others do likewise.

My dream is to start a writing incubator program for senior high and college age students who are interested in writing. I got the idea during when we introduced writing as a career to over 125 high school students at a networking summit. This book is a means to start the next step of my authorpreneurship journey, The Authorpreneurship Project for Youth (TAPY).

MY MISSION

When I was a graduate student at Oral Roberts University, I never imagined that I would become a serious writer, let alone an advocate for the written word and its agents. When we were told to "go into every man's world and spread the Gospel," I did not have a clue that God would use me to be a cheerleader for those who desired to put pen to paper to woo the hearts of readers around the world. I have studied authors and the nuances of the things that make them successful, and compiled my findings in this book and many to come.

My dear authorpreneurs, you have been under close scrutiny in my petri dish for years, and as a result this book is another part of my thesis. I offer it because I love you and greatly admire the courage that you possess in sharing your heart and soul with the world through writing. You are my literary heroes, and this is my tribute to your greatness.

To God be the glory, because without Him, I could do nothing.

Selah

ABOUT THE COMPILER

Sharon C. Jenkins is the Inspirational Principal for The Master Communicator's Writing Services and a senior publishing consultant with Ellechor Media. The Master Communicator's writing services provides business communication services to small businesses, nonprofits, and authors. Sharon is also the mastermind behind the annual Authors Networking Summit (2010–13), America's Favorite Author Competition, and Houston's Favorite Author Competition.

Known as "The Master Communicator," she is proficient in communicating in all forms of media: radio, newspapers, magazines, and spoken word. From 2010–12, she worked as an editor for a major minority communications and marketing company in the fourth largest city in the US. She hosted the Blog Talk Radio Program *The Literary Showcase* from 2010–13. Sharon has moved to the HOA platform and hosts *The Literary Fellowship* on the third Saturday of each month at 10:00 a.m.

Sharon has helped hundreds of authors get their message to the masses through workshops, webinars, her radio show, and coaching. She is currently also a senior publishing consultant for the award-winning Ellechor Publishing House. She has participated in numerous compilations, been a coauthor, and self-published three books. Her solo projects include *Beyond the Closet Door, Christ's Rescue from Abuse* and *Authorpreneurship: The Business Start-Up Manual for Authors*, which is the culmination of everything she has learned from her literary journey and that of other authors. *Will the R.E.A.L. Authorpreneur Please Stand Up?* is her way of celebrating the authors that are the "why" behind her passion to serve them.

For more information about Sharon go to *MCWritingServices.com or SharonCJenkins.com.*

CONTACT INFORMATION

Email: sharon@mcwritingservices.com

Phone: 281-516-8390

Facebook: Facebook.com/iloveauthorpreneurs

Twitter: Twitter.com/Sharon_Jenkins

Google Plus: Plus.Google.com/u/0/+SharonJenkins

LinkedIn: LinkedIn.com/in/SharonCJenkins

Instagram: Instagram.com/SharonCJenkins

Tumblr: Tumblr.com/Blog/TheMasterCommunicator

Join the Authorpreneurship Movement at *MCWritingServices.com/AuthorpreneurSignup* and "Like" our Facebook page at *Facebook.com/Authorpreneurship*!

NOTES

Introduction
1. Red & Black Books – http://redandblackbooks.com

Chapter One—Joel Friedlander
1. *A Self-Publisher's Companion: Expert Advice for Authors Who Want to Publish* – http://www.thebookdesigner.com/companion
2. *The Self-Publishing Roadmap* – http://www.selfpublishingroadmap.com
3. *The Self-Publisher's Ultimate Resource Guide* – http://www.spresourceguide.com

Chapter Two—Matilda Butler
1. Rochelle Carter, *The 7-Step Guide to Authorpreneurship*, pg. 22
2. http://twitter.com/RosiesBandana

3. https://www.facebook.com/RosiesBandana
4. https://www.pinterest.com/RosiesBandana
5. *Writing Alchemy: How to Write Fast and Deep, Memoir Edition* – http://womensmemoirs.com/category/writing-alchemy

Chapter Four—Sharon Norris Elliott

1. Life That Matters Ministries – *http://lifethatmatters.net*
2. Holy Spirit Broadcast Network, "Life That Matters with Sharon Norris Elliott" – *http://HSBN.tv*

Chapter Five—W. Terry Whalin

1. Michael Korda, *Making the List: A Cultural History of the American Bestseller, 1900-1999* – http://amzn.to/1vlPByF
2. Morgan James Publishing info – http://terrylinks.com/mjp1s
3. TerryWhalin.com – http://terrywhalin.com
4. Ask About Book Proposals – http://askaboutproposals.com
5. The Writing Life – http://thewritinglife.ws
6. https://twitter.com/terrywhalin
7. Right Writing News – http://www.right-writing.com/newsletter.html
8. *Jumpstart Your Publishing Dreams* – http://jumpstartdreams.com
9. "Two Words" – http://terrylinks.com/twowords

Chapter Seven—Rochelle Carter

1. "Brand Your Expertise with a Book" Program – http://brandyourexpertisewithabook.com
2. Ellechor Media, LLC – http://ellechormedia.com

Chapter Eight—Nina Amir

1. Authorpreneur: How to Build a Business Around Your Book – http://amzn.to/1vfBAoO

Chapter Eleven—Carla R. Cannon

1. *Women of Standard Magazine* – http://www.womenofstandard.org
2. Carla R. Cannon Enterprises – http://carlacannon.com